Rural Ministry

A parish workbook on lay ministry in the country church

Rural Ministry

A parish workbook on lay ministry in the country church

Leslie J Francis

Keith Littler

and

Jeremy Martineau

with illustrations by
Chris Bishop

First published in February 2000

Acora Publishing
Arthur Rank Centre
Stoneleigh Park
Warwickshire CV8 2LZ

ISBN 0 9516871 6 6

Typesetting by Acora Publishing,
Stoneleigh Park, Warwickshire CV8 2LZ

Printed by
NAC Print Services

Contents

Preface

This book reflects the three authors' firm commitment to and clear confidence in the rural church. We are convinced that planning for the future of the rural church needs both to be grounded in high quality research and to be rooted in local reflection and initiative. *Rural Ministry* is a parish workbook which employs the findings of new research to help local churches reflect on the development of lay ministry to the glory of God.

We wish to record our gratitude to those who have assisted us in preparing this book. First, the organisation of the research has involved many clergy and lay people throughout the rural dioceses of the Church of England and the Church in Wales. Without their help there could have been no book. Second, we record our gratitude to Chris Bishop for enlivening and enriching our words and figures with such entertaining and thought-provoking illustrations. Finally, we record our gratitude to Ros Fane, Anne Rees and Diane Drayson who helped shape the manuscript, and to Katrina Terrance who prepared the camera ready copy.

Leslie J Francis
Keith Littler
Jeremy Martineau

February 2000

Introduction

Rural Anglicanism

Churches in rural areas have undergone some fundamental changes in recent years. Reduction in the number of chapels and churches of the non-conformist traditions has led many people brought up in these traditions to transfer allegiance to other denominations, especially to the Anglican church which may remain the only church building in many rural areas. Increasingly the Anglican church has become the church for all the people and consequently has wanted to embrace a wide range of opinion and practice.

Changes in the structures and resourcing of the rural church have led to fewer full-time stipendiary priests being responsible for larger numbers of churches. Such changes have contributed to the assumption that lay people must be brought into a fuller participation in ministry. The survey reported in this book reveals continuing resistance to that fuller participation.

Further changes in patterns of ministry within the rural church seem inevitable. The one key point made by the present book is that the implementation of change needs to begin by taking seriously the views of those most likely to be affected. The aim of the book, therefore, is to let the views of rural churchgoers be properly heard.

The fullest expression of lay ministry is "in the world" - in the community, at work, in other organisations. This book looks only at the ministry of the laity in the internal functioning of the church as a household of faith.

While researching the views of rural churchgoers we have observed that the role of the clergy in parishes where lay people are taking more responsibility is not diminished but enhanced. Lay people active in ministry ask for more support, teaching and prayer. Clergy will not be redundant in such a church.

Rural Ministry

Rural Ministry is the second volume in a series of parish workbooks designed to help rural churches reflect on their life and mission. The first volume, *Rural Praise*, concentrated on the offering of worship to almighty God. The second volume, *Rural Ministry*, concentrates on the development of lay ministry in the broadest sense within the country church.

There are thirty sections to this workbook. Some churches may decide to use them all. Other churches may wish to select a few examples. Some churches may decide to explore several sections at one time. Other churches may wish to spend longer over a smaller number of sections.

Each section has been drafted in the same way. First, key statistics are presented from a recent survey conducted among two thousand people who attend rural Anglican churches in England and Wales. Then a short reflection on these statistics is followed by questions for local study, and some suggested activities. These activities might well take place away from the normal place of worship, as well as within it.

The survey from which these statistics was taken asked rural churchgoers to rate their 'attitude toward lay people (other than Readers) with appropriate training and accreditation (where appropriate) carrying out' specified aspects of ministry. The aspects of 'ministry' listed in the questionnaire ranged widely from cleaning the church to presiding at the eucharist. The rating used a five point scale from *very negative*, through *neutral* to *very positive*.

Each set of statistics presents four pieces of key information. The pie chart distinguishes between the proportions of rural churchgoers who evaluate the issue as *positive, neutral* and *negative*. Then the statistics examine the relationship between attitude toward lay ministry and three key factors. First the statistics distinguish between the proportions of men and women who evaluate the issue as positive. For example, the table presented in the first section on 'preaching and teaching' demonstrates that 41% of women consider it appropriate for lay people to preach at matins or evensong, compared with 46% of men. Second, the statistics distinguish between the proportions of three age categories who evaluate the issue as positive: the under fifties, those between fifty and sixty-four, and those aged sixty-five and over. For example, the table presented in the first section on 'preaching and teaching' shows that 62% of those under the age of fifty feel positive about lay people giving the address at family services, compared with 49% of those aged sixty-five or over.

Finally the statistics distinguish between the views of those who attend church every week and those who attend church less frequently. For example, the table presented in the first section on 'preaching and teaching' shows that 48% of those who attend church weekly feel positive about lay people preaching at matins or evensong, compared with 33% of those who attend church less frequently.

The questionnaire used to collect this information is printed in the appendix. Some churches may find it helpful to make copies of the questionnaire in order to compile a picture of how their churchgoers feel about these issues.

It is the writers' hope that discussion on these important issues will be carried out apart from the pressure to make policy decisions. Such discussions can then inform and advise those who need to take such decisions. It is to be expected that people will express support on those aspects with which they are most familiar.

Suggestions on using this workbook

To plan a discussion on topics such as these, ensure that participants have the relevant background information in advance. The group may work best with between eight and ten people. To cover such a wide range of viewpoints will require experienced group leadership skills; the function of the group leader is to facilitate discussion, not to impose his or her own views. By modelling listening the leader will enable others to listen. It is important to allow space and time for sharing personal experiences which give rise to present opinions.

The aim of a discussion on any of these topics is to increase knowledge and awareness of some of the issues concerning lay ministry. Sessions should not last more than ninety minutes. At the end of this time participants should have increased their knowledge concerning the breadth of possibilities and the ways in which lay ministry can be developed. They should also be more aware of the origin and formation of their own views and those which others hold. They should have experienced differences as a positive contribution to life in the church.

It is often helpful for refreshments to be served on arrival. The leader or host should ensure that each person is known to everyone. To invite each person to say why they have come may be a useful way of opening the subject. It is more creative to use the time in different ways: working in twos or fours, by brainstorming ideas which are written on a flip chart, by using silence for a time of reflection, and only some time in plenary discussion. It is also important to recognise that extraverts feel much more at home with these group processes than introverts. It is important not to press introverts too hard into contributing in an extravert way. Such pressure may just force them to stay away.

1 Preaching and teaching

Give address at family service

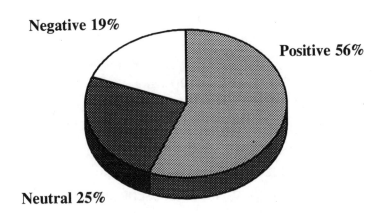

Negative 19%

Positive 56%

Neutral 25%

Positive 56%	
Church attendance	
Sometimes	45%
Weekly	62%
Age	
Under 50	62%
50-64	59%
65 and over	49%
Sex	
Male	55%
Female	56%

Preach at matins or evensong

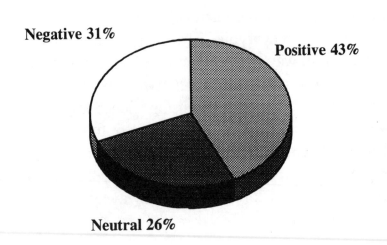

Negative 31%

Positive 43%

Neutral 26%

Positive 43%	
Church attendance	
Sometimes	33%
Weekly	48%
Age	
Under 50	48%
50-64	45%
65 and over	37%
Sex	
Male	46%
Female	41%

Listening to the statistics

- There is more support for lay people giving the address at family services than for lay people preaching at matins or evensong.

- Over half (56%) of rural churchgoers support lay people giving the address at family services.

- Regular churchgoers are more supportive than occasional churchgoers of lay people giving the address at family services.

- Younger churchgoers are more supportive than senior churchgoers of lay people giving the address at family services.

- Men and women share the same views about lay people giving the address at family services.

- Well under half (43%) of rural churchgoers support lay people preaching at matins and evensong.

- Regular churchgoers are more supportive than occasional churchgoers of lay people preaching at matins and evensong.

- Younger churchgoers see more advantages than senior churchgoers in lay people preaching at matins and evensong.

- Men are slightly more in favour than women of lay people preaching at matins and evensong.

Reflection

A central function of teaching and preaching in church is to expound and explain the scriptures; it is the vehicle for direct instruction. It follows that lay people need a sound training in the scriptures and theology in order to preach at matins or evensong or to give the address at family services.

The special value of lay people preaching resides in their knowledge of local affairs and local interests, as well as in the experience of their daily lives. The combination of sound training with local knowledge and secular experience can work to produce valuable and efficient preachers and teachers.

Lay people trained in communication skills may be able to help churches find more appropriate and more effective methods of teaching.

**'When the Vicar trained her in how to preach, he should have stressed
what was <u>really</u> meant by having knowledge of local affairs !'**

Activity

Give a two minute presentation to the rest of the group on a passage of scripture in a style suitable for matins or evensong. Discuss, as a group, how far the presentation explained the passage rather than simply restated it in different words. Repeat the exercise in a style suitable for a family service.

Talking points

- What do you look for in a sermon or an address: instruction, entertainment, enlightenment or spiritual up-lift?

- How well does the voice of the preacher carry in your church? Is a microphone necessary? Are there sound 'flat-spots'?

- How do you feel about children's participation in the family service? Does space permit children's dramatisation of biblical stories?

- Does the structure of the church interior lend itself to the use of an overhead projector or other visual aids?

- What contribution can lay people make to preaching at matins and evensong?

- What contribution can lay people make to organising and/or delivering the address at a family service?

2 Reading the offices

Read lessons at evensong

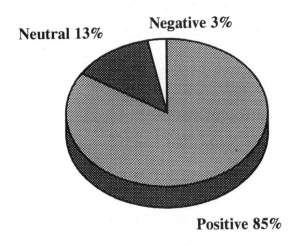

Positive 85%

Church attendance
Sometimes   79%
Weekly   87%

Age
Under 50   86%
50-64   89%
65 and over   80%

Sex
Male   85%
Female   84%

Conduct the service at evensong

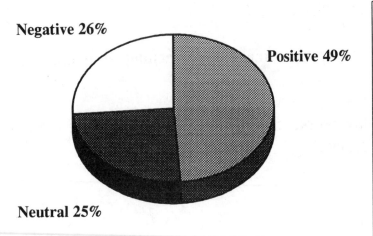

Positive 49%

Church attendance
Sometimes   33%
Weekly   57%

Age
Under 50   50%
50-64   54%
65 and over   44%

Sex
Male   52%
Female   47%

Listening to the statistics

- Considerably more churchgoers approve of lay people reading the lessons at evensong than approve of lay people conducting the service at evensong.

- The vast majority (85%) of rural churchgoers approve of lay people reading the lessons at evensong.

- Regular churchgoers approve more than occasional churchgoers of lay people reading the lessons at evensong.

- Churchgoers in all age groups strongly approve of lay people reading the lessons at evensong but those aged between fifty and sixty-four years are the most supportive.

- Men and women share the same views about lay people reading the lessons at evensong.

- Less than half (49%) of rural church members approve of lay people conducting the service at evensong.

- Regular churchgoers approve more strongly than occasional churchgoers of lay people conducting the service at evensong.

- Churchgoers over the age of sixty-five are less likely than younger churchgoers to approve of lay people conducting the service at evensong.

- Men approve slightly more than women of lay people conducting the service at evensong.

Reflection

The offices of matins and evensong provide a regular opportunity for public worship and can be presented without unnecessary strain or confusion.

The office readings from scripture are, for many people, their main contact with biblical teaching. It is, therefore, important that the presentation of the service is sincere, prayerful and lucid.

Training in presentation and clarity for lay people who read the lessons or who conduct the service is of great importance.

'The sons of Levi: Gershom, Kohath, and Merari. The sons of Kohath: Amram, Iz-har, Hebron, and Uzziel. The children of Amram: Aron, Moses, and Miriam. The sons of Aaron: Nadab, Abihu, Eleazar, and Ithamar. Eleazar was the father of Phine-has of Abishua, Abishua of Bukki, Bukki of Uzzi.......................................

Activity

Read through the services of morning prayer (matins) and evening prayer (evensong) from *The Book of Common Prayer* or *The Alternative Service Book 1980*. Identify the common features and list them, side by side, on a sheet of paper. Consider the significance of each component.

Talking points

• How many people in the parish would be willing to be named in a list of lay people prepared to read the lesson at evensong?

• From where should the lesson be read: the lectern, the choir steps or somewhere else?

• Do some people's voices carry better than others? What should lesson readers do to be heard clearly?

• How do you check the pronunciation of those awkward words that often crop up in the lessons?

• Which parts of the service of evensong can only the priest conduct? What are the implications for lay people when they conduct a service?

• What do you say to a parishioner who suggests that a lay person should not conduct a service of evensong?

3 Word and sacrament

Preside at the eucharist

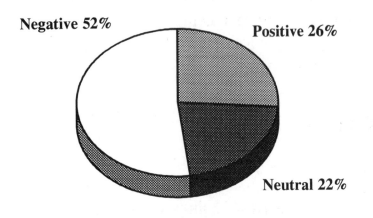

Negative 52%

Positive 26%

Neutral 22%

Positive 26%	
Church attendance	
Sometimes	20%
Weekly	28%
Age	
Under 50	29%
50-64	25%
65 and over	24%
Sex	
Male	24%
Female	27%

Preach at the communion service

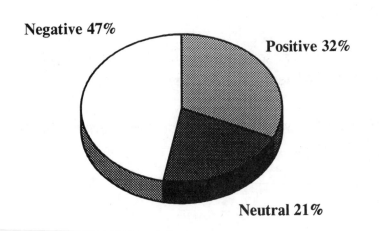

Negative 47%

Positive 32%

Neutral 21%

Positive 32%	
Church attendance	
Sometimes	22%
Weekly	37%
Age	
Under 50	41%
50-64	33%
65 and over	26%
Sex	
Male	33%
Female	31%

Listening to the statistics

- Only one in four (26%) rural churchgoers are supportive of lay people presiding at the eucharist.

- Neither regular nor occasional churchgoers are supportive of lay people presiding at the eucharist.

- Churchgoers under the age of fifty are marginally less opposed to lay people presiding at eucharist than are churchgoers over the age of fifty.

- Men and women share a common opposition to lay people presiding at the eucharist.

- Only one in three (32%) rural churchgoers are supportive of lay people preaching at the communion service.

- Regular churchgoers are more supportive than occasional churchgoers of lay people preaching at the communion service.

- Churchgoers under the age of fifty are notably more supportive than older churchgoers of lay people preaching at the communion service.

- Attitudes to lay people preaching at the communion service are unrelated to gender.

Reflection

To some the parity of word and sacrament would appear to weigh heavily in favour of some form of lay presidency. Yet the tradition of the church has distinguished clearly between the 'licensing' of the lay preacher and the 'ordination' of the president. The former is seen as an administrative procedure and the latter as a liturgical event in the life of the church.

Rural church members clearly uphold the established tradition of presidency by an ordained priest. At the same time rural congregations may now contain people brought up in other traditions more accepting of lay presidency.

Activity

Draw a plan of how you expect the seating arrangements would have been for the Last Supper. Consider Jesus' words at the Last Supper. List the key elements of what Jesus said and what Jesus did. Identify those words and activities retained in the present day eucharist. Identify those words and activities incorporated in the present day eucharist but not recorded in the Last Supper.

Talking points

* What do you believe actually takes place when the Prayer of Thanksgiving is said over the bread and wine?

* How important are the exact words used in the Prayer of Thanksgiving over the bread and wine?

* Is our communion service today a true reflection of what Jesus expects us to do, in his name?

* Is the Prayer of Thanksgiving over the bread and wine more important than the sermon preached at the communion service?

* What experience have you of lay people administering communion from the 'reserved sacrament' either in church or in homes? Is this acceptable?

* Why are only those who are confirmed generally given communion? Why should not all who are baptised be given communion?

4 Eucharistic ministers

Administer chalice at communion

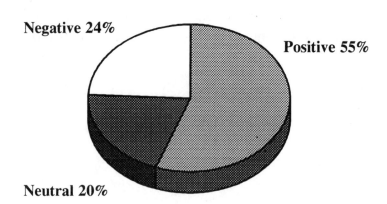

Negative 24%

Positive 55%

Neutral 20%

Positive 55%	
Church attendance	
Sometimes	37%
Weekly	65%
Age	
Under 50	55%
50-64	61%
65 and over	50%
Sex	
Male	59%
Female	53%

Administer bread at communion

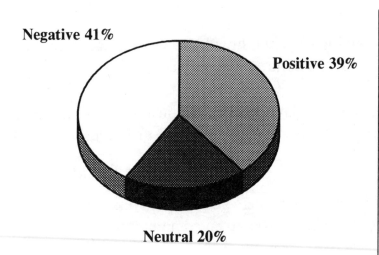

Negative 41%

Positive 39%

Neutral 20%

Positive 39%	
Church attendance	
Sometimes	29%
Weekly	44%
Age	
Under 50	42%
50-64	41%
65 and over	35%
Sex	
Male	41%
Female	37%

Listening to the statistics

- There is more support for lay people administering the chalice at communion than for lay people administering the bread.

- Over half (55%) of rural churchgoers approve of lay people administering the chalice at communion.

- Regular churchgoers are very much more supportive than occasional churchgoers of lay people administering the chalice at communion.

- Churchgoers between the ages of fifty and sixty-four are more supportive of lay people administering the chalice at communion than are churchgoers in both the younger and older age groups.

- Men are slightly more positive than women about lay people administering the chalice at communion.

- Rural churchgoers are almost equally divided over lay people administering the bread at communion, with 41% against and 39% in favour.

- Regular churchgoers are less opposed than occasional churchgoers to lay people administering the bread at communion.

- Older churchgoers are less supportive than younger churchgoers of lay people administering the bread at communion.

- Men are a little more supportive than women of lay people administering the bread at communion.

Reflection

It is common practice for licensed lay people to administer the wine at communion but not to administer the bread. The statistics, therefore, probably reflect rural church members' experiences.

The communion is, by common consent, the most important of all Christian ritual patterns and it would be inappropriate for any aspect of the administration of the bread or the wine to be treated other than with respect for church tradition.

All who administer the bread or the wine should, therefore, be knowledgeable of the purpose and practice of the ritual and remain mindful of the beliefs and sensitivities of those receiving communion.

Activity

In your group, pass round a cup of communion wine and a plate of communion wafers or bread. Write down what you believe to be the difference between the wine and wafers or bread just consumed, and the elements received in the eucharist.

Talking points

- Do you feel any different after you have received communion? If so, why?

- Does it make any difference to the way you feel if you take communion in a different church?

- How do you feel about taking communion in a church of a different denomination from your own?

- Do you feel any different when a lay person gives you communion compared with when a priest gives you communion?

- When lay people assist in the administration of communion, why do they tend to administer the wine rather than the bread?

- Have you attended services where all the lay people administer communion one to another?

5 Proclamation and intercession

Lead intercessions at communion

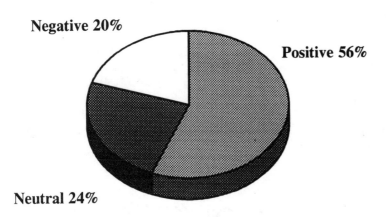

Positive 56%	
Church attendance	
Sometimes	35%
Weekly	67%
Age	
Under 50	61%
50-64	63%
65 and over	46%
Sex	
Male	56%
Female	56%

Read the gospel at communion

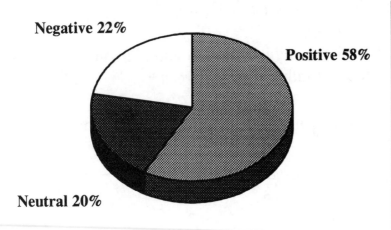

Positive 58%	
Church attendance	
Sometimes	49%
Weekly	63%
Age	
Under 50	62%
50-64	62%
65 and over	52%
Sex	
Male	60%
Female	57%

Listening to the statistics

- Over half (56%) of rural churchgoers value lay people leading the intercessions at communion.

- Regular churchgoers are almost twice as supportive as occasional churchgoers of lay people leading the intercessions at communion.

- Churchgoers over the age of sixty-five are much less supportive than younger churchgoers of lay people leading the intercessions at communion.

- Men and women share the same view about lay people leading the intercessions at communion.

- Over half (58%) of rural churchgoers have a positive view of lay people reading the gospel at communion.

- Regular churchgoers are notably more supportive than occasional churchgoers of lay people reading the gospel at communion.

- Churchgoers over the age of sixty-five are less likely to be supportive of lay people reading the gospel at the communion than are those in younger age groups.

- Men and women hold similar views on lay people reading the gospel at communion.

Reflection

It is common practice in many places for the intercessions to be led by lay people at the communion service. If intercessions are to be personalised with the names of the sick and the bereaved, it is important for intercession leaders to liaise closely with the rest of the pastoral team. Failure to do so may not only be the cause of embarrassment and hurt for those whose names have been omitted but may also separate the intercessions from the life of the worshipping community.

It is less common in some places for lay people to read the gospel at the communion service. When lay people are invited to read the gospel at the communion service this provides another clear indication of shared ministry among the people of God.

'Let us pray for the dire economic situation that is facing our country at the moment.
Let us pray for peace in the many troubled areas of the world.
Let us pray for social justice in our inner city areas.
Let us pray for all who are on hospital waiting lists.
Let us pray for the people who live in 'Cherry Blossom Close......the odd numbers'.

Activity

Prepare prayers of intercession for a communion service and consider to whom the prayers are directed, God or the congregation. What should be included and what should be excluded? After all, we cannot pray for everything and everybody all of the time. Or can we?

Talking points

- Do you think that it is best if the person who preaches at the communion service also reads the gospel? Why?

- Do the congregation members at the communion service normally perceive any notable difference between the readings from the Old Testament, the Epistles and the Gospels? If so, how are the differences interpreted?

- Would you feel that a lay person is the best person to lead the intercessions at the communion service? If so, why?

- Do you feel that it is right to personalise the intercessions with the names of the sick and the bereaved? Or do you see problems in this practice?

6 Visiting the sick

Take communion to the sick

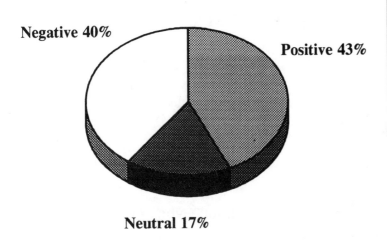

Negative 40%

Positive 43%

Neutral 17%

Positive 43%	
Church attendance	
Sometimes	29%
Weekly	50%
Age	
Under 50	44%
50-64	43%
65 and over	42%
Sex	
Male	43%
Female	43%

Visit the sick at home

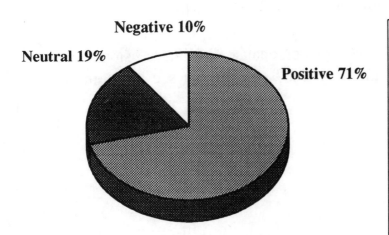

Negative 10%

Neutral 19%

Positive 71%

Positive 71%	
Church attendance	
Sometimes	57%
Weekly	77%
Age	
Under 50	73%
50-64	73%
65 and over	67%
Sex	
Male	69%
Female	72%

 # Listening to the statistics

- There is considerably more support for lay people visiting the sick at home than for lay people taking communion to the sick.

- Less than half (43%) of rural churchgoers believe it is appropriate for lay people to take communion to the sick.

- Regular churchgoers are nearly twice as likely as occasional churchgoers to approve of lay people taking communion to the sick.

- Age makes very little difference to how rural churchgoers feel about lay people taking communion to the sick.

- Men and women hold similar attitudes to lay people taking communion to the sick.

- Nearly three quarters (71%) of rural church members are supportive of lay people visiting the sick at home.

- Regular churchgoers are much more supportive than occasional churchgoers of lay people visiting the sick at home.

- Senior churchgoers are slightly less supportive of lay people visiting the sick at home than are younger churchgoers.

- Men and women are almost equally positive about lay people visiting the sick at home.

Reflection

Clergy in rural areas tend to have responsibility for parishioners scattered over extensive geographical areas. In these circumstances visiting sick people at home can be difficult and lay support is essential. Indeed, in rural areas there is often a tradition of people caring for neighbours and this should be encouraged, cultivated and deemed part of normal parish activity. Whilst the parish priest will wish to visit sick people at home, reliance must rest upon lay people to ensure that parishioners feel properly supported by the church in times of sickness.

Taking communion to the sick by lay people implies that the bread and wine have been previously consecrated by the priest. Some people find 'communion by extension' unsatisfactory. One recent writer has (perhaps unfairly) described the process of 'communion by extension' as totally mechanistic and almost superstitious. Others see this as a positive way to include in the Sunday celebration of communion those who are unable to be present at the service. For some elderly or disabled people communion at home may be the only way they can participate in the worship of the local church.

'Drop me off……..I'll be with Mrs Smithers for 10 minutes……….then hoist me up and take me over to Little Snoddling…..'

Activity

Draw up a list of everyone in the community who is ill, whether at home or in hospital. Consider their needs and list these needs under the headings 'practical needs', 'social needs' and 'spiritual needs'. Then consider how best these needs can be met.

Talking points

- What sort of things do people need when they are sick and housebound: shopping, conversation, transport?

- What did you find most difficult when you were sick?

- Do you feel that communion at home is important when you are sick or are other things, like someone calling for a conversation, more important?

- How do we find out when people in the neighbourhood are sick and need help?

- Is anyone responsible for letting the clergy know when people in the parish are sick?

- Is it helpful to organise a team of visitors, or should we each look after our nearest neighbours?

- Is 'communion by extension' practised in your parish? Should it be?

7 Hospitals and residential homes

Visit elderly in residential homes

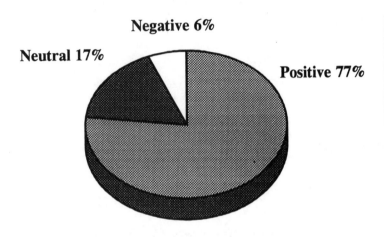

Negative 6%

Neutral 17%

Positive 77%

Positive 77%	
Church attendance	
Sometimes	69%
Weekly	82%
Age	
Under 50	80%
50-64	80%
65 and over	73%
Sex	
Male	75%
Female	79%

Visit parishioners in hospital

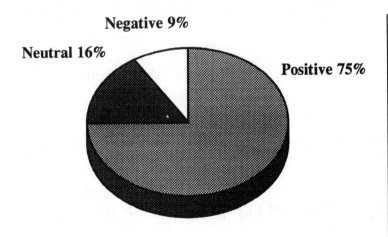

Negative 9%

Neutral 16%

Positive 75%

Positive 75%	
Church attendance	
Sometimes	64%
Weekly	81%
Age	
Under 50	76%
50-64	78%
65 and over	71%
Sex	
Male	73%
Female	76%

Listening to the statistics

- More than three quarters (77%) of rural churchgoers are in favour of lay people visiting elderly people in residential homes.

- Churchgoers of all ages are in favour of lay people visiting elderly people in residential homes although those aged sixty-five and over are a little less supportive than are those in younger age groups.

- Men and women share similarly positive views on lay people visiting elderly people in residential homes.

- Three quarters (75%) of rural churchgoers hold a positive attitude to lay people visiting parishioners in hospital.

- Eight in ten regular churchgoers are in favour of lay people visiting parishioners in hospital compared with six in ten occasional churchgoers.

- Churchgoers aged sixty-five and over hold a slightly less favourable attitude to lay people visiting parishioners in hospital than do younger churchgoers.

- Men and women hold an almost equally positive attitude to lay people visiting parishioners in hospital.

Reflection

These days, hospital stays are often short and rural clergy sometimes find it difficult to visit parishioners before they are discharged. Lay visitors are, therefore, greatly to be welcomed.

In the case of elderly people in residential homes, lay visitors can often give more time than the clergy to listen and converse. Lay people are more likely to share a common background with the people they are visiting and are more able to reminisce with them in a way that is helpful to many elderly people.

Lay visitors to hospitals and residential homes are also frequently able to provide transport for the spouses and friends of those whom they are visiting.

When undertaking visiting on behalf of the church, lay people are engaging in a professional aspect of ministry and benefit from proper and adequate training to prepare them for what may be expected of them.

**'No way am I visiting St Placids Day Centre again.
They've only formed a Chapter of Hell's Grannies !'**

Activity

Plan a simple series of interviews or a questionnaire to find out what elderly people in residential homes miss most. Use the results to reflect on how your church might respond to their needs.

Talking points

- Is it possible to organise a list of car owners prepared to convey people to the hospital for visits or appointments?

- What are the benefits of visiting people in hospital?

- What are the problems of visiting people in hospital?

- Is it helpful to organise 'nostalgic' visits to residential homes for the elderly, where you take photographs of bygone days, for example?

- What are the dangers to watch for when visiting elderly people in residential homes?

8 Bereavement

Visit bereaved before the funeral

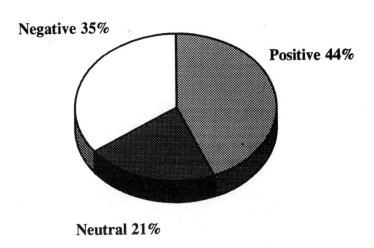

Negative 35%

Positive 44%

Neutral 21%

Positive 44%

Church attendance	
Sometimes	32%
Weekly	51%
Age	
Under 50	47%
50-64	46%
65 and over	41%
Sex	
Male	44%
Female	44%

Visit bereaved after the funeral

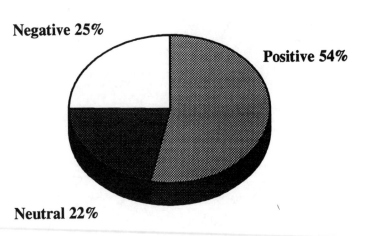

Negative 25%

Positive 54%

Neutral 22%

Positive 54%

Church attendance	
Sometimes	39%
Weekly	61%
Age	
Under 50	57%
50-64	57%
65 and over	49%
Sex	
Male	52%
Female	55%

Listening to the statistics

- Rural churchgoers believe it is more appropriate for lay people to visit the bereaved after the funeral than before the funeral.

- Rural churchgoers have mixed views about lay people visiting the bereaved before the funeral, 44% indicating approval and 35% indicating disapproval.

- More regular churchgoers (51%) than occasional churchgoers (32%) approve of lay people visiting the bereaved before the funeral.

- Senior churchgoers are slightly less inclined to approve of lay people visiting the bereaved before the funeral than are younger churchgoers.

- Views about lay people visiting the bereaved before the funeral are unrelated to gender.

- Over half (54%) of rural churchgoers value lay people visiting the bereaved after the funeral.

- Regular churchgoers are much more inclined than occasional churchgoers to value lay people visiting the bereaved after the funeral.

- Churchgoers aged sixty-four and under are more supportive of lay people visiting the bereaved after the funeral than are churchgoers aged sixty-five and over.

- Men and women hold similar views on lay people visiting the bereaved after the funeral.

Reflection

It is natural for friends and neighbours to visit the bereaved both before and after a funeral. It is, however, in the days, weeks and months following the funeral that the lay visitor can be of particular support in helping the bereaved come to terms with their loss.

Even so, bereavement counselling can be difficult for both counsellor and counselled. Training is necessary if such a role is to be undertaken in a professional sense by lay people in the name of the church.

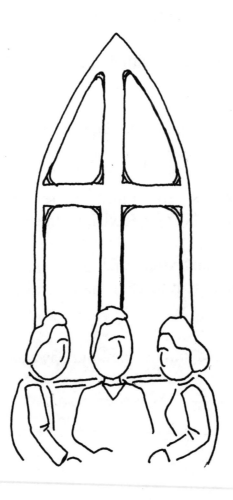

Activity

Invite participants to discuss in pairs or groups of three their own experience of bereavement and what they looked for most from the church. Consider how adequately their needs were met.

This activity may not be appropriate if a member of the group has experienced bereavement too recently.

Talking points

- What are people's first and most immediate needs when they experience bereavement?

- What can we do to help?

- What are people's main needs in the weeks following the funeral?

- What can we do to help?

- Do you need to be a 'special sort of person' to visit those who are bereaved?

- Would professional training improve the help you could offer to the bereaved?

9 Work with children

Run a mid-week children's club

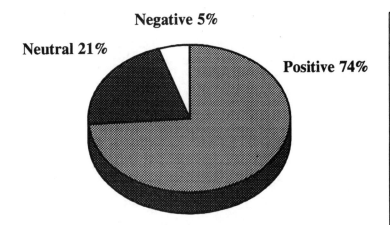

Negative 5%

Neutral 21%

Positive 74%

Positive 74%	
Church attendance	
Sometimes	70%
Weekly	76%
Age	
Under 50	81%
50-64	80%
65 and over	63%
Sex	
Male	73%
Female	75%

Teach in Sunday school

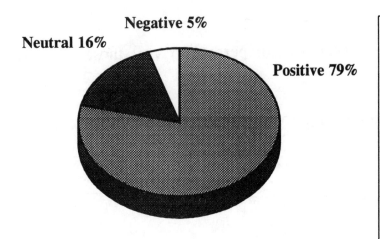

Negative 5%

Neutral 16%

Positive 79%

Positive 79%	
Church attendance	
Sometimes	72%
Weekly	83%
Age	
Under 50	80%
50-64	83%
65 and over	74%
Sex	
Male	80%
Female	79%

Listening to the statistics

- Rural churchgoers welcome lay people running a mid-week children's club.

- More than three quarters (76%) of regular churchgoers and 70% of occasional churchgoers support lay people running a mid-week children's club.

- Enthusiasm for lay people running a mid-week children's club is especially marked among those aged sixty-four and under.

- Men and women are equally supportive of lay people running a mid-week children's club.

- Rural churchgoers place high emphasis on lay people teaching in Sunday school.

- Over four fifths (83%) of regular churchgoers and 72% of occasional churchgoers are supportive of lay people teaching in Sunday school.

- Enthusiasm for lay people teaching in Sunday school is especially marked among those aged sixty-four and under.

- Men and women are equally supportive of lay people teaching in Sunday school.

Reflection

There are long established and widespread practices of lay people conducting Sunday school and running other church groups for children, including Brownies, Guides, Cubs, Scouts and many others.

Many lay people will have had training as school teachers or youth club leaders, and will bring professional skills to their role as Sunday school teacher or children's club leader.

Safeguards, however, must be imposed upon all who work with children in the parish to ensure that children are protected from any risk of abuse or exploitation. To this end, each parish should have in place a child protection policy and work within the guidelines offered by the diocese or national church for vetting and checking those who volunteer to work among children and young people.

'The P.C.C. decided to allow the Sunday School to have a go at abseiling'

Activity

Arrange to visit a local primary school and observe the material displayed, the structure of the timetable, the range of subjects taught and the children at play. Invite the school to display some of the children's work in the church. Invite the diocesan children's adviser to discuss this area of work.

Talking points

- What materials do you need to run a Sunday school, or a mid-week club for children?

- Where can these materials be obtained?

- What skills do you need to run a Sunday school or a mid-week club for children?

- What checks and protective measures do you need to put in place to ensure that those working with children and young people do not abuse the privilege?

- Are the physical facilities provided by your church or church hall suitable for Sunday school or children's clubs? How can the facilities be best utilised or modified?

- What training is available for Sunday school teachers and for leaders of children's clubs?

10 Leading groups

Lead a house discussion group

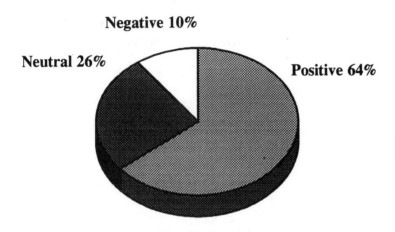

Negative 10%

Neutral 26%

Positive 64%

Positive 64%	
Church attendance	
Sometimes	51%
Weekly	72%
Age	
Under 50	72%
50-64	69%
65 and over	55%
Sex	
Male	63%
Female	66%

Lead youth work

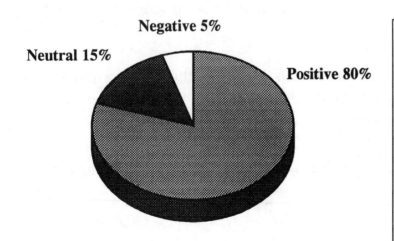

Negative 5%

Neutral 15%

Positive 80%

Positive 80%	
Church attendance	
Sometimes	75%
Weekly	83%
Age	
Under 50	84%
50-64	83%
65 and over	76%
Sex	
Male	80%
Female	80%

Listening to the statistics

- More rural churchgoers hold a positive view of lay people leading youth work than leading house discussion groups.

- Well over half (64%) of rural churchgoers regard positively lay people leading house discussion groups, although a quarter (26%) are indifferent and 10% are opposed.

- Regular churchgoers are considerably more in favour than occasional churchgoers of lay people leading house discussion groups.

- Rural churchgoers aged sixty-five and over are much less inclined to hold a positive view of lay people leading house discussion groups than are younger churchgoers.

- Men and women show similar levels of support for lay people leading house discussion groups.

- Rural churchgoers place strong emphasis on lay youth work leaders, with 80% showing support and only 5% indicating opposition.

- Both regular and occasional churchgoers are strongly in favour of lay youth work leaders.

- There is strong support for lay youth work leaders from churchgoers of all age groups.

- Both men and women strongly endorse lay youth work leaders.

Reflection

Youth work is especially important in some rural areas where activities for young people may be limited. It is, however, a specialist role that does not come easily to everyone. Training and vetting youth leaders is essential if the work with youth is to be successful and project a Christian ethos.

House groups, properly conducted, can be a vital agent for combining social and spiritual support throughout the parish. The successful house group can bring small groups of parishioners together for prayer, study, discussion and social activities.

Leaders of house groups may well need help in:
*   establishing clear aims and objectives for house group meetings;
*   providing suitable material for group discussion;
*   developing skills of leading and stimulating discussion;
*   feeding back their successes and failures to other house group leaders.

'What experience do you think you need to engage in youth work ?'

'Well, for a start, you need a working knowledge of Bus Stops !'

Activity

Arrange to visit a youth club or uniformed youth organisation. Observe the activities and talk to the leaders. Discover from young people living in the parish how they spend their leisure time and what facilities they would like to help to develop in the community.

Talking points

- What skills and experiences do people need to engage in youth work?

- Is it possible to organise house groups in your area? If so, is transport needed to help people meet in one another's homes?

- What would be the aims and objectives of organising house groups in your area?

- What sort of topics and materials would keep people interested and involved in a house group?

- What training is available for youth leaders? Would people be prepared to train? Who would fund the training?

- What help could be provided by the diocesan youth work adviser?

11 Preparation for sacraments

Prepare adults for confirmation

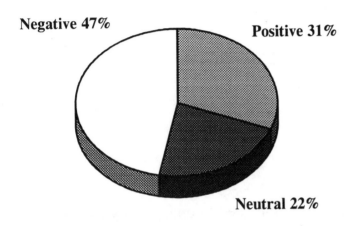

Negative 47%
Positive 31%
Neutral 22%

Positive 31%	
Church attendance	
Sometimes	23%
Weekly	34%
Age	
Under 50	38%
50-64	31%
65 and over	25%
Sex	
Male	34%
Female	28%

Prepare those to be married

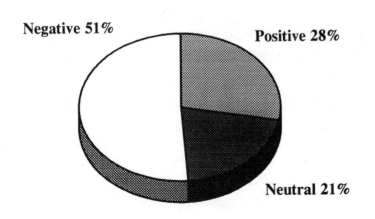

Negative 51%
Positive 28%
Neutral 21%

Positive 28%	
Church attendance	
Sometimes	20%
Weekly	32%
Age	
Under 50	34%
50-64	30%
65 and over	22%
Sex	
Male	28%
Female	27%

Listening to the statistics

- There is more opposition (47%) to lay people preparing adults for confirmation than there is support (31%).

- Only a third of regular churchgoers hold a positive attitude to lay people preparing adults for confirmation.

- Less than a quarter of occasional churchgoers hold a positive attitude to lay people preparing adults for confirmation.

- Churchgoers aged under fifty are the least likely to be opposed to lay people preparing adults for confirmation.

- Women hold a slightly more negative view than men about lay people preparing adults for confirmation.

- Little more than a quarter of rural churchgoers are in favour of lay people preparing those to be married.

- Less than one in three regular churchgoers are in favour of lay people preparing those to be married.

- Only one in five occasional churchgoers are in favour of lay people preparing those to be married.

- Senior churchgoers are even more negative than younger churchgoers about lay people preparing those to be married.

- Both men and women are equally opposed to lay people preparing those to be married.

Reflection

Although the statistics indicate lack of support for lay people to be involved in the preparation of adults for confirmation and also in preparing those to be married, lay people have much to offer in these contexts.

Working closely with the clergy, lay people can bring varied experiences to discussions with adults, both in respect of confirmation and marriage.

Lay people's experiences and the difficulties they had to face in coming to confirmation as an adult, in their understanding of participation in the eucharist, in the personal problems they have had to overcome in their own relationships, can give very valuable support to the clergy as they prepare adults, whether for confirmation or marriage.

'As my seventh wife was always saying to me……..'

Activity

List on a sheet of paper some of the key issues to be addressed in the preparation of adults for confirmation. Share experiences on how such issues can be addressed. List on a sheet of paper some of the key problems faced by married couples. Share experiences of how such problems can be faced and overcome.

Talking points

- It is often said that as soon as young people are confirmed they stop coming to church. Is this true in your parish?

- How can your church help confirmed young people and adults to remain in touch?

- Do you think it is better to be confirmed as children, teenagers or adults?

- There is a high level of divorce and marriage breakdown in our society. Why do you think this is?

- How important is preparation for marriage in today's society?

- How can your church help to prepare people for married life?

12 Occasional offices

Funeral of church person

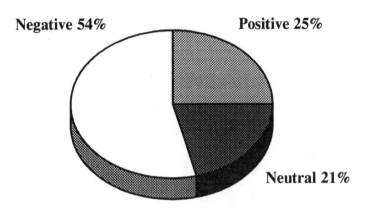

Negative 54%   **Positive 25%**

Neutral 21%

Positive 25%	
Church attendance	
Sometimes	18%
Weekly	29%
Age	
Under 50	24%
50-64	25%
65 and over	27%
Sex	
Male	28%
Female	24%

Baptise infants

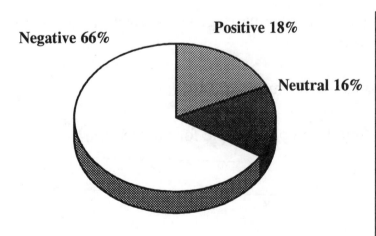

Negative 66%   **Positive 18%**

Neutral 16%

Positive 18%	
Church attendance	
Sometimes	13%
Weekly	21%
Age	
Under 50	17%
50-64	18%
65 and over	19%
Sex	
Male	19%
Female	17%

Listening to the statistics

- Over half (54%) of rural churchgoers are opposed to a lay person conducting the funeral of a church person.

- Only one in four rural churchgoers are in favour of a lay person conducting the funeral of a church person.

- Regular churchgoers are somewhat less negative than occasional churchgoers about a lay person conducting the funeral of a church person.

- Age makes little difference to attitudes to a lay person conducting the funeral of a church person.

- Neither men nor women are convinced about the appropriateness of a lay person conducting the funeral of a church person.

- Rural churchgoers are overwhelmingly opposed to lay people baptising infants with only 18% registering positive support.

- Although regular churchgoers are a little less negative than occasional churchgoers about lay people baptising infants, the level of support remains low (21%).

- Attitudes to lay people baptising infants are unrelated to age.

- Men and women are equally opposed to lay people baptising infants.

Reflection

Although the church permits lay people, in certain circumstances, to conduct baptisms and funerals, most church members would, it seems, prefer these services to be conducted by clergy.

It may be helpful to establish the role of lay people more clearly in these services by inviting lay leaders to share leadership with the clergy. Lay people can also assist with readings and prayers. Indeed, the support of a lay person in this capacity can often be greatly appreciated by those concerned.

A CLOSE FAMILY BAPTISM

Activity

Gather around the font in church and read through the baptism service from the new service book. Consider what the service entails and discuss how the leadership can be most effectively shared with the lay people.

Invite the undertaker to give a talk about the funeral practices of different churches and denominations. Consider how the leadership of funerals can be most effectively shared with lay people.

Talking points

- Do you feel that baptism is treated seriously by parents? Do Godparents treat their role seriously?

- What is the role of a Godparent? Do Godparents need help and training for their role?

- How important is it to personalise a funeral by including details of the life of the deceased?

- Do you feel that there should be any real difference between a funeral service in church and a funeral service at the crematorium?

- What should be included in a service at the deceased person's home if it is before the service in church?

- What should be included in a service at the deceased person's home if it is instead of a service in church?

- How do you feel about 'Green Funerals'? Who should conduct the service?

13 Managing the church school

Church primary school governor

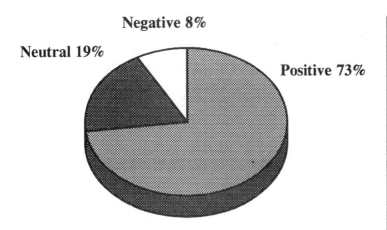

Negative 8%

Neutral 19%

Positive 73%

Positive 73%		
Church attendance		
Sometimes	68%	
Weekly	76%	
Age		
Under 50	77%	
50-64	77%	
65 and over	67%	
Sex		
Male	78%	
Female	70%	

Chair church school governors

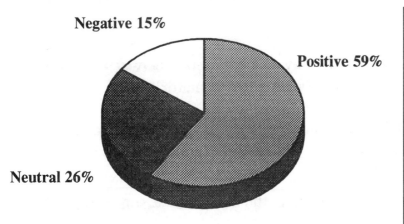

Negative 15%

Positive 59%

Neutral 26%

Positive 59%		
Church attendance		
Sometimes	52%	
Weekly	63%	
Age		
Under 50	63%	
50-64	63%	
65 and over	53%	
Sex		
Male	65%	
Female	56%	

Listening to the statistics

- There is more support for lay people being governors of church primary schools than for a lay person actually chairing church school governors.

- Nearly three quarters (73%) of rural churchgoers support lay people being governors of church primary schools.

- Only 8% of rural churchgoers are opposed to lay people being governors of church primary schools.

- Those aged sixty-five and over are somewhat less convinced than younger churchgoers about lay people being governors of church primary schools.

- Men are even more in favour than women of lay people being governors of church primary schools.

- Three fifths (59%) of rural churchgoers support a lay person chairing church school governors.

- Regular churchgoers are more in favour than occasional churchgoers of a lay person chairing church school governors.

- Those aged sixty-five and over are somewhat less convinced than younger churchgoers about a lay person chairing church school governors.

- Men see more advantages than women in a lay person chairing church school governors.

Reflection

Many lay people bring valuable experience from industry and business to church school governing bodies, often having expertise in chairing and conducting meetings.

Training and support is offered to school governors by local education authorities as well as by the church. Both lay people and clergy should be encouraged to undertake such opportunities to develop their effectiveness as school governors.

It is important for the governors of church schools appointed by the church to promote the church-related ethos of the school.

**'No doubt we benefit from his work-a-day-world experience,
but I would have thought sewage workers washed before meetings !'**

Activity

Arrange for a governor of a local school or representative of the local education authority to provide information about the duties and responsibilities of a school governor. Consider how school management has changed in recent years.

Talking points

- Church schools need Christian people to influence their management and organisation. How do you feel you can help?

- In what ways and to what extent should the church influence a church school in the parish?

- What has the church got to offer the church school?

- What has the church school got to offer the church?

- Church schools need appropriately experienced Christian people to chair governing bodies. How do you feel you can help?

- Are you prepared to become involved in the training programme for governors offered by local education authorities or by the church?

14 Supporting the church school

Church visitor to primary school

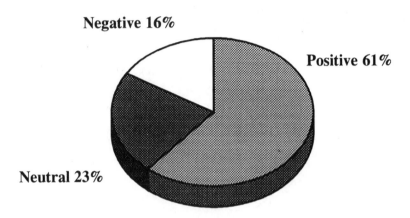

Negative 16%

Positive 61%

Neutral 23%

Positive 61%	
Church attendance	
Sometimes	50%
Weekly	66%
Age	
Under 50	67%
50-64	65%
65 and over	52%
Sex	
Male	62%
Female	59%

Church primary school assembly

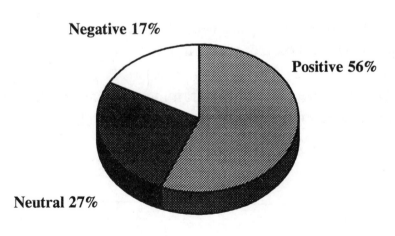

Negative 17%

Positive 56%

Neutral 27%

Positive 56%	
Church attendance	
Sometimes	46%
Weekly	61%
Age	
Under 50	63%
50-64	61%
65 and over	46%
Sex	
Male	56%
Female	56%

Listening to the statistics

- Well over half (61%) of rural churchgoers hold a positive attitude to a lay person being a visitor to a church primary school.

- Regular churchgoers are notably more positive (66%) than occasional churchgoers (50%) about a lay person being a visitor to a church primary school.

- Younger churchgoers are more likely to see advantages in a lay person being a visitor to a church primary school than are senior churchgoers.

- Men and women share a similar opinion on a lay person being a visitor to a church primary school.

- Over half (56%) of rural church members regard positively a lay person taking assembly in a church primary school.

- Regular churchgoers are notably more in favour (61%) than occasional churchgoers (46%) of a lay person taking assembly in a church primary school.

- Younger churchgoers are more likely to see advantages in a lay person taking assembly in a church primary school than are senior churchgoers.

- Men and women share a similar opinion on a lay person taking assembly in a church primary school.

Reflection

Lay people can bring interesting and varied personal experience and knowledge to a church primary school. They can support and assist the school in a variety of ways.

Current legislation states that worship in church schools should reflect the traditions of the school's trust deed. In other words the school assembly provides a proper link between the life of the school and the life of the local church. This offers a key opportunity for clergy and for lay people, but one which requires careful thought and training.

Primary schools are increasingly security conscious and visitors to a primary school are generally required to wear an identifying badge, to report to the office or headteacher on arrival, to be aware that the school entrance gate may be locked during school hours, and to be formally registered as someone in contact with children in a church primary school.

**'Personally, I think it is easier to get into heaven
than into our own village school!'**

Activity

Invite a church school to provide a display of children's work to be exhibited in the church. Offer the school a display about the work of your church.

Talking points

- What experience, knowledge or artifacts do you have that would be of interest to the children in the local church school?

- Would the experience, knowledge or artifacts contribute to the school assembly?

- Could you help to bring information about the Christian year to the school assembly?

- In what other ways could you help the local church school as a visitor?

- Would involvement in the assembly help to strengthen links between church and school.

- What checks would you expect to be applied to prevent the 'wrong people' getting access to schools?

15   Understanding the county school

County primary school governor

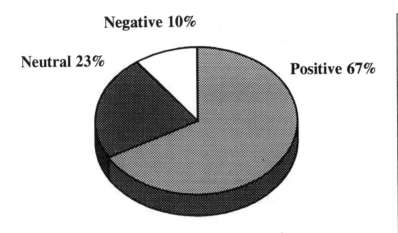

Negative 10%

Neutral 23%

Positive 67%

Positive 67%	
Church attendance	
Sometimes	60%
Weekly	71%
Age	
Under 50	70%
50-64	74%
65 and over	58%
Sex	
Male	71%
Female	64%

County primary school assembly

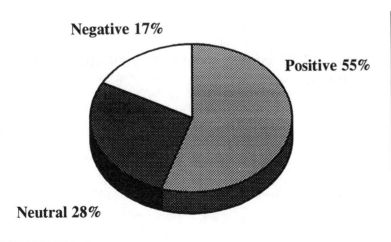

Negative 17%

Positive 55%

Neutral 28%

Positive 55%	
Church attendance	
Sometimes	45%
Weekly	61%
Age	
Under 50	61%
50-64	59%
65 and over	48%
Sex	
Male	56%
Female	55%

Listening to the statistics

- Two thirds (67%) of rural churchgoers are in favour of lay people being governors of a county primary school.

- Regular churchgoers are even more in favour (71%) than occasional churchgoers (60%) of lay people being governors of a county primary school.

- Churchgoers aged sixty-five and over are less in favour of lay people being governors of a county primary school than are churchgoers in younger age groups.

- Men are more in favour than women of lay people being governors of a county primary school.

- Over half (55%) of rural churchgoers are positive about lay people taking assembly in a county primary school.

- Regular churchgoers approve more strongly than occasional churchgoers of lay people taking assembly in a county primary school.

- Younger churchgoers are more positive than older churchgoers about lay people taking assembly in a county primary school.

- Gender makes little difference to opinions on lay people taking assembly in a county primary school.

Reflection

Since there is no obligation for a county primary school to invite local clergy or lay church members to the assembly, it is a privilege when clergy or lay church members are involved in taking assemblies. Such involvement can create important links between a county primary school and a local church.

The same may be said about the lay person as governor of a county primary school. Links between church and school can be of benefit to both.

NUTTLESFORD CHRONICLE

'There were great celebrations at Noddle Parish Church last night, following the announcement that the Vicar had been invited to take an assembly at the village school, our reporter..........'

Activity

Invite the local county primary school to create a display of children's work to exhibit in the church. Discover if some of the classes would like to visit the church to see their work displayed and to learn about the building and the people who worship there.

Talking points

- What contact does your church have with local county primary schools?

- Do members of your church serve as governors of local county primary schools?

- What has the church to offer county primary schools?

- What have county primary schools to offer the church?

- What role is it appropriate for the church to play in county primary schools?

- Discuss again the checks for ensuring that the 'wrong people' are not given access to the school. How can protection be applied in such a way that the children are safeguarded, but people from the community can bring their skills and knowledge into the school?

16 Parish administration

Keep the parish records

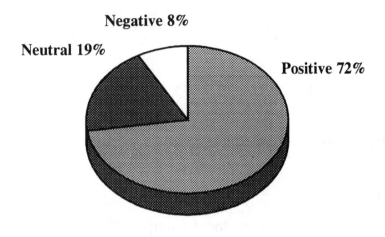

Positive 72%

Church attendance	
Sometimes	66%
Weekly	75%
Age	
Under 50	73%
50-64	77%
65 and over	68%
Sex	
Male	76%
Female	70%

Administer rotas

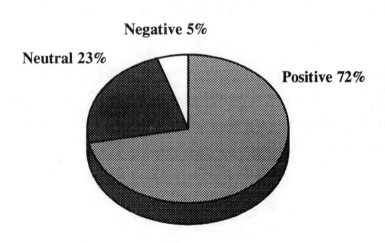

Positive 72%

Church attendance	
Sometimes	66%
Weekly	75%
Age	
Under 50	76%
50-64	76%
65 and over	65%
Sex	
Male	75%
Female	69%

 # Listening to the statistics

- Rural churchgoers hold a positive attitude to lay people keeping the parish records.

- Regular churchgoers are even more supportive than occasional churchgoers of lay people keeping the parish records.

- Rural churchgoers of all ages are in favour of lay people keeping the parish records but those aged between fifty and sixty-four are the most supportive.

- Men are more supportive than women of lay people keeping the parish records.

- Rural churchgoers hold a predominantly positive attitude to lay people administering rotas.

- Three quarters (75%) of regular churchgoers are supportive of lay people administering rotas, while the figure for occasional churchgoers is somewhat lower (66%).

- Although those aged sixty-five and over are the least supportive of lay people administering rotas, it remains that 65% are in favour.

- Men are more supportive than women of lay people administering rotas.

Reflection

It is important that parish records are kept diligently and accurately. Since not all clerics have the aptitude, interest or time to keep careful records, there is a sound case for involving the skills and enthusiasm of lay people who may well bring relevant experience from business and commerce.

With any voluntary organisation the administration of rotas requires care and sensitivity. It can be time consuming to ensure that all participants are happy with the rotas and feel that their contribution is properly valued.

**'Vicar, may I introduce Abraham Dredge.
He's a walking parish record.'**

Activity

Look up old records of baptisms, marriages and burials and consider the value and importance of record keeping. Look up records of service rotas in old parish magazines and consider how far they are adjusted to suit local rural needs.

Talking points

- Have parish boundaries and church groupings changed for your community? Does this mean that some of the parish records are kept elsewhere?

- How complete is the set of records kept in the church?

- Is it worth seeking to complete the missing records? How would you go about this?

- Would providing details of family histories serve as a source of fund-raising for the parish?

- How far would involvement in preparing service rotas create beneficial links between clergy and lay ministers, between lay ministers from different churches within your group of parishes, or between lay ministers and congregation?

17 Parish finance

Record church covenants

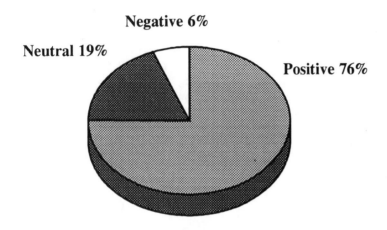

Negative 6%

Neutral 19%

Positive 76%

Positive 76%	
Church attendance	
Sometimes	69%
Weekly	79%
Age	
Under 50	75%
50-64	82%
65 and over	70%
Sex	
Male	79%
Female	74%

Organise fundraising

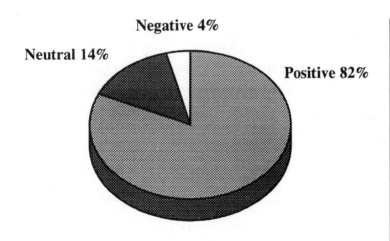

Negative 4%

Neutral 14%

Positive 82%

Positive 82%	
Church attendance	
Sometimes	78%
Weekly	85%
Age	
Under 50	84%
50-64	87%
65 and over	77%
Sex	
Male	83%
Female	83%

Listening to the statistics

- A substantial majority (76%) of rural churchgoers approve of a lay person recording the church covenants.

- Four fifths (79%) of regular churchgoers and 69% of occasional churchgoers approve of a lay person recording the church covenants.

- Churchgoers aged between fifty and sixty-four indicate the strongest support for a lay person recording the church covenants (82%).

- Those aged sixty-five and over are the least certain about a lay person recording the church covenants (70%).

- Men are even more supportive than women of a lay person recording the church covenants.

- The vast majority (82%) of rural churchgoers approve of lay people organising fundraising.

- Regular churchgoers are even more convinced than occasional churchgoers about lay people organising fundraising.

- Churchgoers aged between fifty and sixty-four indicate the strongest approval of lay people organising fundraising (87%).

- Those aged sixty-five and over are the least certain about lay people organising fundraising.

- Men and women hold a similarly positive view of lay people organising fundraising.

Reflection

Lay people can bring a breadth of ideas to fundraising, gained from life experiences.

Lay people who have worked in finance often appreciate the value of covenants and the tax returns involved, far better than clerics and are generally better placed to commend these ideas to the congregation.

By definition, fundraising will involve broad sections of the public, extending beyond the immediate members of the church.

In many areas the work of the local church may attract more voluntary giving than any other charitable cause.

'To raise funds, the neighbouring parish kidnapped the Vicar and demanded £500 for his release.
What happened?
The PCC paid up £1,000 and asked the kidnapping parish to keep him!'

Activity

Prepare a balance sheet to estimate expenditure and income each year for the next five years. Reflect on where savings can be made and how new income can be generated.

Talking points

- What are the usual fundraising activities in your parish? Could these be extended? In what ways?

- What are the monies raised needed for? Are they used for essential expenditure or to provide items which would not otherwise be available?

- What are the financial benefits to the church of asking people to covenant their contributions or to use gift aid? Does this work equally well for those who are employed and for those who are retired?

- Are there advantages in separate fundraising strategies for the church building and for the ministry of the church?

18 Parochial Church Council

Chair church council meeting

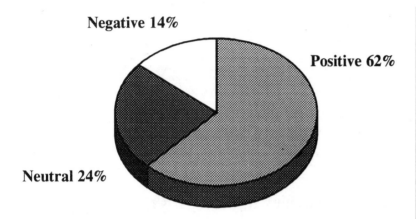

Negative 14%

Positive 62%

Neutral 24%

Positive 62%	
Church attendance	
Sometimes	53%
Weekly	66%
Age	
Under 50	61%
50-64	67%
65 and over	57%
Sex	
Male	67%
Female	57%

Minute church council meetings

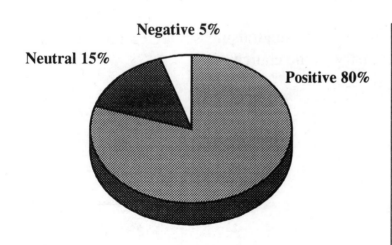

Negative 5%

Neutral 15%

Positive 80%

Positive 80%	
Church attendance	
Sometimes	75%
Weekly	82%
Age	
Under 50	81%
50-64	84%
65 and over	74%
Sex	
Male	82%
Female	78%

Listening to the statistics

- There is more support for lay people minuting the church council meeting than for lay people chairing the church council meeting.

- A lay person chairing the church council meeting is welcomed by 62% of rural churchgoers.

- Regular churchgoers are more inclined to approve of a lay person chairing the church council meeting (66%) than are occasional churchgoers (53%).

- Senior churchgoers are the least convinced about a lay person chairing the church council meeting.

- Men are more supportive than women of a lay person chairing the church council meeting.

- Eight in ten rural churchgoers welcome a lay person minuting the church council meeting.

- Over four fifths (82%) of regular churchgoers and three quarters (75%) of occasional churchgoers approve of a lay person minuting the church council meeting.

- Senior churchgoers hold a slightly less positive view of a lay person minuting the church council meeting than do younger churchgoers.

- Both men and women hold positive views on a lay person minuting the church council meeting.

Reflection

The Parochial Church Council is an important body, charged with the functions of promoting the whole mission of the church (pastoral, evangelistic, social and ecumenical) in the parish. It is concerned with the preparation of a parish budget, the review of clergy expenses and other important matters.

Such a significant body should draw upon the best possible expertise available in the parish.

The position of chairperson is an important one and demands special skills - skills as likely to be found in lay people as in clergy. A lay chairperson can free the cleric to engage more freely in discussion and debate.

'I think the new chairman is taking his responsibilities a mite too seriously.'

Activity

Prepare an audit of parish needs, setting out those things which you feel require attention, whether it be the renovation of the church building, the establishment of a youth club, the organisation of house groups, a luncheon club for the elderly, or the like. Rank order the items you have identified.

Talking points

- How often does the Parochial Church Council (PCC) meet? Does it have a wide representation of parish members? If not, would a change of meeting times help?

- Are all members helped to make a useful contribution to the discussion at PCC meetings? If not, how could the situation be improved?

- Do you prefer the clergy to chair PCC meetings, or is it better to have a lay chairperson?

- Are minutes of PCC meetings made available for all church members to see and discuss?

- Who controls the preparation of the agenda for PCC meetings? Do you feel that some important items are excluded from the agenda? How could this be changed?

19 Parish magazine

Distribute the magazine

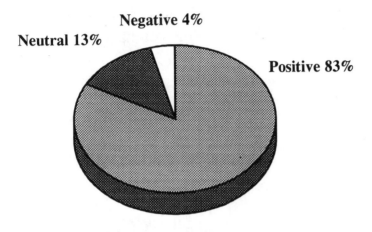

Positive 83%

Positive 83%	
Church attendance	
Sometimes	80%
Weekly	85%
Age	
Under 50	83%
50-64	87%
65 and over	80%
Sex	
Male	84%
Female	83%

Edit the parish magazine

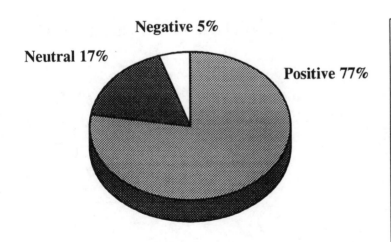

Positive 77%

Positive 77%	
Church attendance	
Sometimes	73%
Weekly	79%
Age	
Under 50	80%
50-64	84%
65 and over	70%
Sex	
Male	80%
Female	76%

Listening to the statistics

- High emphasis is placed by rural churchgoers on lay people distributing the parish magazine.

- Only 4% of rural churchgoers hold a negative view of lay people distributing the parish magazine.

- Both regular and occasional churchgoers are strongly in favour of lay people distributing the parish magazine.

- Those aged between fifty and sixty-four are the most supportive of lay people distributing the parish magazine.

- Men and women hold equally positive views on lay people distributing the parish magazine.

- More than three quarters (77%) of rural churchgoers regard positively the parish magazine being edited by a lay person.

- Only 5% of rural churchgoers hold a negative view of the parish magazine being edited by a lay person.

- Both regular and occasional churchgoers support the parish magazine being edited by a lay person.

- Those aged between fifty and sixty-four are the most positive about the parish magazine being edited by a lay person.

- Men are marginally more inclined than women to support the parish magazine being edited by a lay person.

Reflection

The parish magazine can be a vital form of outreach for the church, bringing the message of the gospel to people who do not attend services. It is important, therefore, that the parish magazine should strive for high standards of content and presentation. Every effort should be made to distribute the parish magazine as widely as possible. The wider the circulation, the greater is the need for lay involvement in distributing, organising, collecting fees, seeking advertisers, and encouraging others to contribute to the contents.

'I agree a new magazine was needed for everyone in the parish, but having a centre fold page spread of the Vicar's wife on the beach at Flotsum-on-Sea is a bit much!'

Activity

Draft a new style parish magazine. Identify the key items for inclusion and consider at which age group each item is aimed. Discuss the aims and objectives of each item. Consider whether changes should be made to the content and style of the current parish magazine.

Talking points

- What do you think should be included in a parish magazine? Should there be general items of 'social' interest as well as 'religious' items?

- Should the parish magazine be aimed most specifically at non-church attenders or at church attenders?

- How important are graphics? Who in the parish has appropriate computer facilities for graphics?

- Should the parish magazine be subsidised or pay its way?

- Should the parish magazine be professionally produced and printed?

- Is there merit, in a rural area, of joining forces with neighbouring parishes to produce a benefice or deanery magazine?

20 Pastoral care

Pray for people in the parish

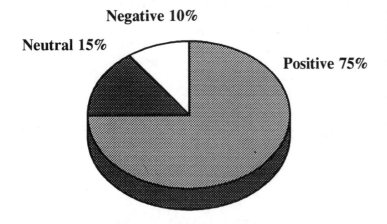

Negative 10%

Neutral 15%

Positive 75%

Positive 75%	
Church attendance	
Sometimes	61%
Weekly	82%
Age	
Under 50	81%
50-64	78%
65 and over	69%
Sex	
Male	73%
Female	77%

Hold confidential conversation

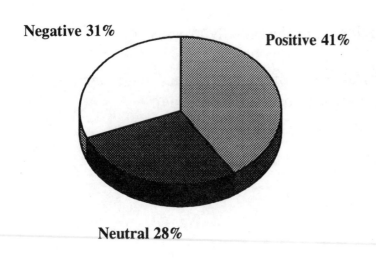

Negative 31%

Positive 41%

Neutral 28%

Positive 41%	
Church attendance	
Sometimes	27%
Weekly	49%
Age	
Under 50	49%
50-64	46%
65 and over	31%
Sex	
Male	43%
Female	40%

Listening to the statistics

- There is much more support for a lay person praying for people in the parish than for lay people to hold confidential conversation with parishioners.

- Three quarters (75%) of rural church members believe it is appropriate for lay people to pray for people in the parish.

- Regular churchgoers are notably more inclined than occasional churchgoers to find it appropriate for lay people to pray for people in the parish.

- Younger churchgoers see greater value in lay people praying for people in the parish than do senior churchgoers.

- Women are marginally more inclined than men to hold a positive view of lay people praying for people in the parish.

- Only four in ten rural churchgoers believe it is appropriate for lay people to hold confidential conversation with parishioners.

- Three in ten rural churchgoers are opposed to lay people holding confidential conversation with parishioners.

- Occasional churchgoers are much more uncertain than regular churchgoers about lay people holding confidential conversation with parishioners.

- Churchgoers aged sixty-five and over are the most doubtful about the appropriateness of lay people holding confidential conversation with parishioners.

- Men and women holds similar views about the appropriateness of lay people holding confidential conversation with parishioners.

Reflection

Keeping confidences is not easy. Clergy and lay people who engage in this form of ministry on behalf of the church require adequate training and subsequent adherence to proper professional standards. Moreover, individuals who exercise such a ministry of listening or counselling themselves need a professional supervisor who can support them in their ministry.

It is a mark of the caring Christian community with a good level of spirituality that lay people and clergy should pray for each other. Many people, however, need help and support in developing not only a right attitude to prayer, but also an understanding of what the concept of prayer entails. An underdeveloped theology of intercessory prayer can lead to inappropriate expectations.

'And this morning we pray for
Mrs Torrington and her piles.
For Mr Norrish and his recurring problem, which we are all well aware of,
and a special thought for Miss Trump after her particularly
embarrassing experience late last night outside the fish and chip shop'

Activity

Draw a plan of the parish. Consider the practicality of sub-dividing the parish into streets, districts or geographical areas as the basis for a disciplined pattern of prayer.

Talking points

- In some rural areas, many families are related and movement of people is minimal. What are the problems of lay persons holding confidential conversation in this context?

- Do you find that some parishioners are unlikely to talk to non-family members about personal and confidential issues?

- Do you see value in a prayer group coming together to pray for the local community? Do you see any dangers in such activity?

- How do you feel about others praying for you?

- What sort of things should be included when we pray for others in our community? What sort of things should be excluded?

21 Concern for the community

Organise care scheme in village

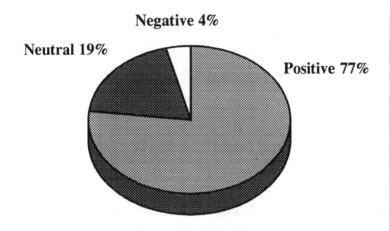

Positive 77%

Church attendance
Sometimes	74%
Weekly	78%

Age
Under 50	81%
50-64	82%
65 and over	69%

Sex
Male	78%
Female	76%

Organise lunch club for elderly

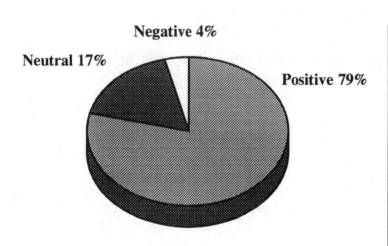

Positive 79%

Church attendance
Sometimes	77%
Weekly	80%

Age
Under 50	81%
50-64	84%
65 and over	73%

Sex
Male	78%
Female	80%

Listening to the statistics

- Over three quarters (77%) of rural churchgoers see value in lay people organising a care scheme in the village.

- Only 4% believe it is inappropriate for lay people to organise a care scheme in the village.

- A positive view of lay people organising a care scheme in the village is held by regular and occasional churchgoers.

- Those aged sixty-five and over are less positive than younger churchgoers about lay people organising a care scheme in the village.

- Men and women are equally supportive of lay people organising a care scheme in the village.Over three quarters (79%) of rural churchgoers see value in lay people organising a lunch club for the elderly.

- Only 4% believe it is inappropriate for lay people to organise a lunch club for the elderly.

- Regular and occasional churchgoers are almost equally in favour of lay people organising a lunch club for the elderly.

- While senior churchgoers claim to be the least enthusiastic about lay people organising a lunch club for the elderly, it remains that 73% give their support.

- Men and women give almost equal approval to lay people organising a lunch club for the elderly.

Reflection

Lunch clubs for the elderly and village care schemes satisfy important community needs and also provide valuable Christian outreach. Through such activities, the church can minister to many who do not attend church services. It may be counter-productive, however, if the church is perceived as forcing a denominational or religious view upon people at lunch clubs and care schemes.

Lay leadership of care schemes and lunch clubs for the elderly can often benefit from collaboration with other voluntary organisations like the WRVS and from cooperation with the statutory social services.

The Diocesan Board for Social Responsibility may be able to help develop a proper response to local community needs.

Dear P.C.C Secretary,
I agree that the Lunch Club is a good idea,
but dressing all the waitresses in clerical
collars is a little pointed don't you think ?

Yours

Activity

Map the parish, identifying the homes of people over sixty years of age. Consider the transport implications of bringing people from a rural community to a central place for a lunch club or for social activities.

Talking points

- Is there a central meeting place in the parish where a lunch club or other social activities could be held?   What are the transport implications of getting people to a central meeting place in a rural community?

- Given the specific demands on people's lifestyle in rural areas, are there particular days or times when a lunch club or care scheme would operate most successfully?

- Would it be possible to cooperate with other bodies, like WRVS and the statutory social services, to provide a lunch club for the elderly?

- A care scheme can mean many things.   What does it mean to you? What purpose would it serve and to whom would it be directed in your parish?

22 Developing fellowship

Serve coffee after the service

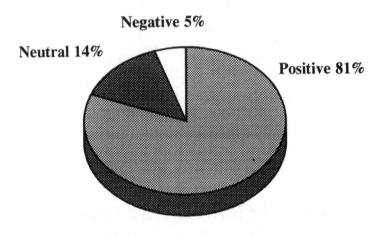

Positive 81%		
Church attendance		
Sometimes		75%
Weekly		85%
Age		
Under 50		84%
50-64		86%
65 and over		75%
Sex		
Male		82%
Female		81%

Organise church social programme

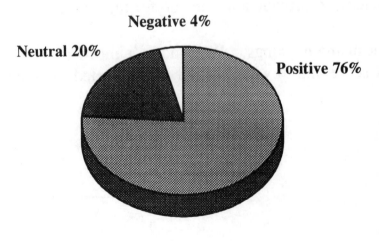

Positive 76%		
Church attendance		
Sometimes		70%
Weekly		79%
Age		
Under 50		80%
50-64		82%
65 and over		68%
Sex		
Male		77%
Female		76%

Listening to the statistics

- The vast majority (81%) of rural churchgoers place high emphasis on lay people serving refreshments after the service.

- Regular churchgoers are more appreciative than occasional churchgoers of lay people serving refreshments after the service.

- Younger churchgoers look even more favourably on lay people serving refreshments after the service than senior churchgoers.

- Men and women are equally supportive of lay people serving refreshments after the service.

- Three quarters (76%) of rural churchgoers welcome lay people organising the church social programme.

- Regular churchgoers are somewhat more appreciative than occasional churchgoers of lay people organising the church social programme.

- Senior churchgoers indicate the least support for lay people organising the church social programme.

- Men and women hold similar views on lay people organising the church social programme.

Reflection

It is important that the church has a social life. Many people welcome the opportunity to converse with one another after the service in church as well as to have an opportunity to meet with the clergy.

Serving refreshments after a service depends, of course, on either the availability of an adjacent hall or the provision of facilities within the church itself. Most churches can make sufficient provision and this can lead to other aspects of the church's social activities.

Lay organisation is essential if use is to be made of local talents with respect to (say) organising a parish cricket team, pantomime, excursion, barbecue, firework display and so on.

Activity

Consider how the population of the parish divides into different identifiable groups, say by age and sex. Consider the social and recreational interests of people within these different groups.

Talking points

- How much should the church be involved in social activities?

- Does your church have the facilities to serve refreshments after the service? Will people remain after the service? Will the clergy be present?

- What social activities are possible in the parish?

- Can fund-raising be linked to some social activities? Is it helpful to do so?

- Which age groups would benefit most from parish social activities?

- Is there a noticeable need in the parish to bring people together for social events?

- What are some of the difficulties of arranging social functions in a rural parish?

23 Ministry of welcome

Contact newcomers in parish

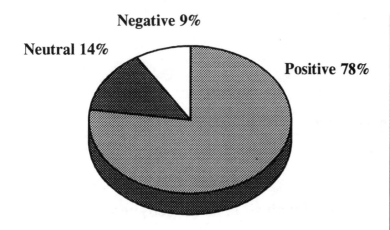

Positive 78%

Church attendance
Sometimes   65%
Weekly   84%

Age
Under 50   78%
50-64   81%
65 and over   75%

Sex
Male   78%
Female   78%

Welcome visitors and tourists

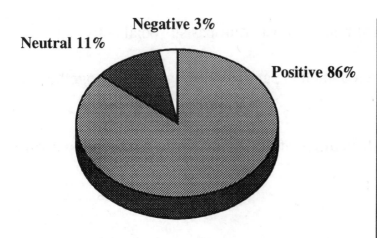

Positive 86%

Church attendance
Sometimes   80%
Weekly   89%

Age
Under 50   88%
50-64   90%
65 and over   82%

Sex
Male   86%
Female   86%

Listening to the statistics

- Over three quarters (78%) of rural churchgoers are positive about lay people contacting newcomers in the parish.

- Regular churchgoers place particularly high emphasis on lay people contacting newcomers in the parish.

- Occasional churchgoers see notably less value in lay people contacting newcomers in the parish.

- Churchgoers of all ages hold a positive view of lay people contacting newcomers in the parish.

- Men and women are equally supportive of lay people contacting newcomers in the parish.

- The vast majority (86%) of rural churchgoers approve of lay people welcoming visitors and tourists.

- Regular churchgoers are even more supportive than occasional churchgoers of lay people welcoming visitors and tourists.

- Age makes only a slight difference to levels of support for lay people welcoming visitors and tourists.

- Men and women are equally supportive of lay people welcoming visitors and tourists.

Reflection

It is a common criticism of churches that visitors are not made welcome. It is important that the congregation as a whole is mindful of the needs of visitors. Often clergy need to hurry off to another service and it is left to lay people to help visitors feel that their presence was welcome in the church.

When new people move into a parish, a visit from the clergy is often appreciated, but it is the informal contact of neighbours that may be most influential in determining whether a new family wants to become part of the local church.

Holiday areas present additional challenges. Some holiday-makers seek a break from their normal routine, including church attendance, and have little desire to be contacted by the local church. Others may have a strong need of the church during their temporary stay as holiday-makers. It is important, therefore, that they are provided with information in their holiday accommodation about local church services and other church-based points of contact.

**At his Visitation the Rural Dean made note that
the Church Notice Board was somewhat out of date.**

Activity

Prepare statistics to show numbers of people moving into the parish in the last year, the number of family visitors, and the number of holiday visitors. Consider how the church might best minister to these people.

Talking points

- How should newcomers be welcomed to the parish? How useful are letters, personal visits, invitations to social events or invitations to church?

- Is there a danger of putting off newcomers by contacting them too soon?

- How should tourists be welcomed? How useful are public notices or leaflets available in holiday accommodation?

- How can the children of newcomers and tourists be made welcome? Does the church offer any facilities for children who are new to the parish?

- How attractive and useful are the church noticeboards for newcomers, visitors and tourists?

- Does your diocese have an officer for tourism? How can such a post be fully developed?

- What help is available from the National Churches Tourism Group?

24 The church as resource

Lock and unlock the church

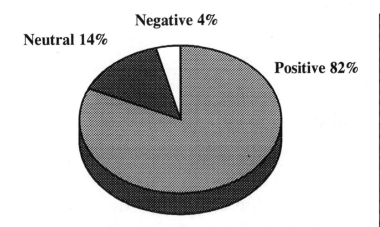

Positive 82%		
Church attendance		
Sometimes		78%
Weekly		83%
Age		
Under 50		82%
50-64		85%
65 and over		78%
Sex		
Male		83%
Female		80%

Oversee church security

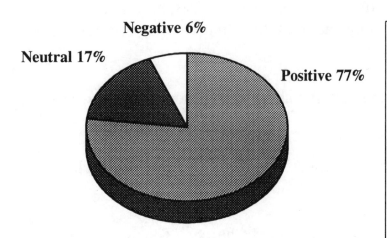

Positive 77%		
Church attendance		
Sometimes		72%
Weekly		79%
Age		
Under 50		77%
50-64		82%
65 and over		72%
Sex		
Male		81%
Female		73%

Listening to the statistics

- The vast majority (82%) of rural churchgoers approve of lay people having responsibility for locking and unlocking the church.

- Only 4% are opposed to lay people having responsibility for locking and unlocking the church.

- Both regular and occasional churchgoers are in agreement about the acceptability of lay people having responsibility for locking and unlocking the church.

- All age groups approve of lay people having responsibility for locking and unlocking the church.

- Both men and women approve of lay people having responsibility for locking and unlocking the church.

- Over three quarters (77%) of rural churchgoers approve of lay people overseeing church security.

- Only 6% are opposed to lay people overseeing church security.

- Occasional churchgoers are somewhat less certain than regular churchgoers about lay people overseeing church security.

- Senior churchgoers are somewhat less certain than younger churchgoers about lay people overseeing church security.

- Women are somewhat less certain than men about lay people overseeing church security.

Reflection

Because the vicarage is likely to be located some distance from many rural churches, it is necessary that there is a keyholder near the church. Many rural churches are now unlocked in the morning and locked up again in the evening. This allows both parishioners and visitors to use the church for prayer and meditation as well as for sightseeing. When churches are kept locked during the day, it is important that local people and visitors are informed how they can gain access. It is also important that churches are opened in good time for the Sunday services.

'He's always locked the church—living in the Tower obviously helps'

Activity

Prepare a basic church guide. This could be a simple A4 sheet indicating the main points of historic interest and main things to see. Review the security issues associated with the church.

Talking points

- Has your church organised a 'Church Watch Scheme'?

- Do visitors have easy access to the church? Is there a keyholder living near the church? Do notices in the church porch tell people where they can get a key?

- Are any valuable items left accessible in the church, or are they locked away when not in use?

- Is the insurance cover adequate for liability for accidents to visitors, damage to the building and loss of valuables?

- Who has overall responsibility for security in your church?

25 Taking care of the church

Clean the church

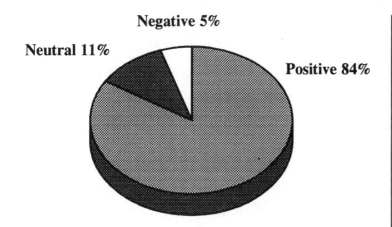

Negative 5%

Neutral 11%

Positive 84%

Positive 84%	
Church attendance	
Sometimes	80%
Weekly	86%
Age	
Under 50	86%
50-64	88%
65 and over	80%
Sex	
Male	87%
Female	82%

Cut the churchyard grass

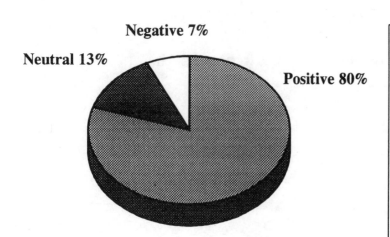

Negative 7%

Neutral 13%

Positive 80%

Positive 80%	
Church attendance	
Sometimes	77%
Weekly	82%
Age	
Under 50	82%
50-64	84%
65 and over	75%
Sex	
Male	82%
Female	79%

 # Listening to the statistics

- The majority (84%) of rural churchgoers have a positive attitude to lay people cleaning the church.

- Occasional churchgoers are a little less certain than regular churchgoers about lay people cleaning the church.

- Senior churchgoers are somewhat less convinced about lay people cleaning the church than are younger churchgoers.

- A slightly higher proportion of men than women agree that the church should be cleaned by lay people.

- The majority (80%) of rural churchgoers have a positive attitude to lay people cutting the churchyard grass.

- Occasional churchgoers are a little less certain than regular churchgoers about lay people cutting the churchyard grass.

- Senior churchgoers are somewhat less convinced about lay people cutting the churchyard grass than are younger churchgoers.

- Similar proportions of men and women approve of lay people cutting the churchyard grass.

Reflection

Few small rural churches are able to afford the cost of paid cleaners and grass cutters and, therefore, depend heavily on volunteers.

It is important that churchyards are kept tidy, out of respect for those who rest there and its environmental quality. It is also important that the interior of the church is kept clean and tidy to provide a proper context for worship.

Many parish councils contribute to the cost of maintaining the churchyard.

**'I've been exploring in the churchyard.
Until now I've only ever seen Pygmies on the telly!'**

Activity

Conduct a survey into parishioners' attitudes toward the churchyard. Do they have views on the standards to which it should be maintained? Do they have views on whose responsibility it is to maintain the churchyard? Use the replies to evaluate your church's policy on churchyard maintenance.

Talking points

•   Is there a cleaning rota for the church? Are the same people always doing the cleaning? Is it necessary or wise to involve more people in this activity?

•   Does the church provide the cleaning materials? Can cleaners get easy access to the church?

•   Is there a grass cutting rota for the churchyard? Are the same people always doing the grass cutting?

•   Is the church responsible for providing a mower or strimmer? Is it serviced regularly? Is there insurance against accident? Is the mower or strimmer kept in the church? Does it provide a fire risk?

26 Keeping up appearances

Arrange flowers in church

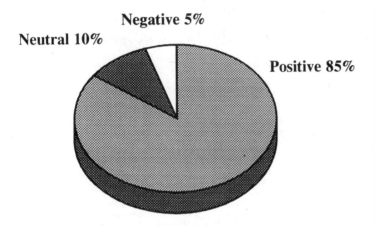

Negative 5%

Neutral 10%

Positive 85%

Positive 85%		
Church attendance		
Sometimes		82%
Weekly		87%
Age		
Under 50		87%
50-64		88%
65 and over		81%
Sex		
Male		84%
Female		86%

Take care of church embroidery

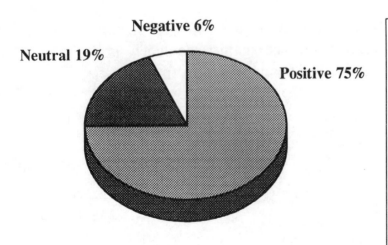

Negative 6%

Neutral 19%

Positive 75%

Positive 75%		
Church attendance		
Sometimes		70%
Weekly		77%
Age		
Under 50		79%
50-64		80%
65 and over		68%
Sex		
Male		76%
Female		75%

Listening to the statistics

- The vast majority (85%) of rural churchgoers welcome lay people arranging the flowers in church.

- Occasional churchgoers are slightly less convinced than regular churchgoers about lay people arranging the flowers in church.

- A high proportion of churchgoers in all age groups welcome lay people arranging the flowers in church.

- Men and women are more or less equally enthusiastic about lay people arranging the flowers in church.

- Three quarters (75%) of rural churchgoers regard positively lay people taking care of church embroidery.

- Occasional churchgoers are slightly less convinced than regular churchgoers about lay people taking care of church embroidery.

- Senior churchgoers are notably less positive about lay people taking care of church embroidery than are younger churchgoers.

- Men and women are equally supportive of lay people taking care of church embroidery.

Reflection

It is common practice for lay people to take responsibility for both the flowers in church and the embroidery. Sometimes ways need to be found to help other people engage in these activities without upsetting the people who have helped in this way for a long time.

Flowers and embroidered cloths can be used to symbolise liturgical times in the church's calendar and, if pursued sensitively by lay people and clergy in partnership, can be a source of learning about the Church's year as well as enjoyment in the intrinsic value.

**'I see the Vicar's wife has taken this suggestion of a display
of church linen seriously.'**

Activity

Make a display of all the church's linen. Review what needs to be repaired or replaced. Arrange a flower festival and try to involve new people in this activity.

Talking points

- Who is responsible for the flowers in your church?

- Why are flowers brought into church?

- What do you like best about flowers in church?

- When are flowers not appropriate in church?

- Who is responsible for the linen and embroidery in your church?

- Why are linen and embroidery used in church?

- What do you like best about church linen, embroidery and vestments?

- When are embroidery and vestments not appropriate in church?

27 Church music

Play organ or other instruments

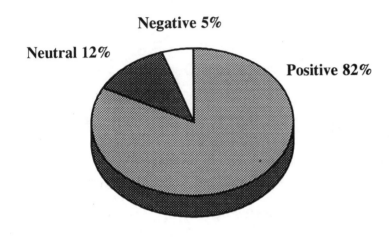

Negative 5%

Neutral 12%

Positive 82%

Positive 82%	
Church attendance	
Sometimes	79%
Weekly	84%
Age	
Under 50	84%
50-64	87%
65 and over	77%
Sex	
Male	83%
Female	82%

Choose hymns/songs for worship

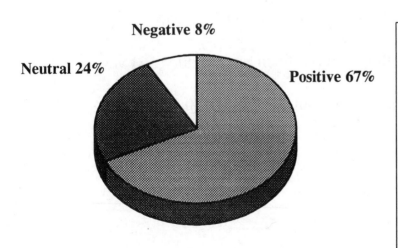

Negative 8%

Neutral 24%

Positive 67%

Positive 67%	
Church attendance	
Sometimes	62%
Weekly	70%
Age	
Under 50	73%
50-64	70%
65 and over	61%
Sex	
Male	63%
Female	70%

Listening to the statistics

- There is more support for lay people playing the organ or other musical instruments in church than for lay people actually choosing the hymns/songs for worship.

- Only 5% of rural churchgoers are opposed to lay people playing the organ or other musical instruments in church.

- Regular churchgoers are slightly more in favour than occasional churchgoers of lay people playing the organ or other musical instruments in church.

- Younger churchgoers hold an even more positive view of lay people playing the organ or other musical instruments in church than do senior churchgoers.

- Both men and women regard positively lay people playing the organ or other musical instruments in church.

- Two thirds (67%) of rural church members are positive about lay people choosing the hymns/songs for worship, while a quarter are indifferent and only 8% are opposed.

- Regular churchgoers are more positive than occasional churchgoers about lay people choosing the hymns/songs for worship.

- Younger churchgoers are more supportive of lay people choosing the hymns/songs for worship than are those aged sixty-five and over.

- Woman are more positive than men about lay people choosing the hymns/songs for worship.

Reflection

Although rural churches can often manage perfectly well without musical accompaniment, the organ or other musical instrument is perceived by many as an important aid to worship. The range of hymns is generally extended by a competent accompanist. Background music can produce an atmosphere of ease and prayerfulness.

Responsibility for choosing the hymns can be fraught with dangers and disagreements between lay musicians and clergy. It is important that this is approached in partnership to ensure the best possible relevance of the music to the other aspects of the service, including the theme of bible readings.

Many churches draw on a wide range of musical skills in addition to playing the organ.

**'They tried to find out if there was any musical talent to help
lead the hymn singing. All they got was Mr Hogweed and his triangle.'**

Activity

Discover the range of musical instruments played by members of the local church and other local residents. Arrange a Songs of Praise service demonstrating how different songs or hymns can be accompanied by different instruments.

Talking points

* Would the present organist welcome help from young musicians in the service?

* Are there young people living locally who would like to learn to play the organ?

* What advice on church music can be obtained locally, from the diocese, or from national bodies?

* Could links be created with the local school's music department?

* Would the church be prepared to help fund training someone to play the organ or other musical instrument?

* Is the church able to employ a Director of Music?

* How adequate/appropriate is the hymn book(s) used in your church?

28 Performing arts

Sing in the church choir

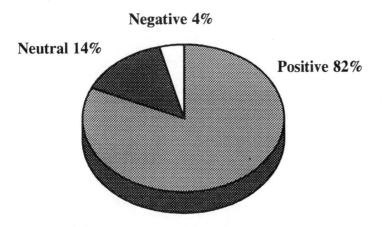

Negative 4%

Neutral 14%

Positive 82%

Positive 82%	
Church attendance	
Sometimes	77%
Weekly	85%
Age	
Under 50	84%
50-64	85%
65 and over	78%
Sex	
Male	83%
Female	82%

Perform in church drama group

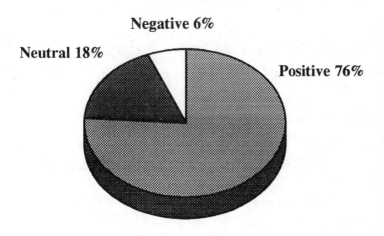

Negative 6%

Neutral 18%

Positive 76%

Positive 76%	
Church attendance	
Sometimes	71%
Weekly	78%
Age	
Under 50	81%
50-64	80%
65 and over	68%
Sex	
Male	75%
Female	76%

Listening to the statistics

- Only 4% of rural churchgoers disapprove of lay people singing in the church choir.

- More than three quarters of both regular and occasional churchgoers regard positively lay people singing in the church choir.

- Senior churchgoers hold a slightly less positive view of lay people singing in the church choir than do younger churchgoers.

- Men and women hold similarly positive attitudes to lay people singing in the church choir.

- Three quarters (76%) of rural church members see advantages in lay people performing in a church drama group.

- Regular churchgoers are slightly more positive than occasional churchgoers about lay people performing in a church drama group.

- Younger churchgoers are more positive about lay people performing in a church drama group than are senior churchgoers.

- Men and women hold similarly positive attitudes to lay people performing in a church drama group.

Reflection

Belonging to a choir, even in a small rural church, is often beneficial to the individual members because of the sense of belonging and group support. The choir may serve as a link between worship and social functions. Performing in a church drama group can have similar benefits for the individual. In both cases, the choir and the drama group may prove to be the catalyst that brings young people into the otherwise alien world of the worship of the church. It can also help church members to take the otherwise alien world of the worship of the church out into the community.

**'Tonight's Senior Youth Club's re-enactment of the story of
David and Bathsheba is a sell out.'**

Activity

Work with the local school to arrange a pantomime, concert or drama presentation to be held in the church. Explore how the building can best be used for such events. It may be helpful to rearrange the seating.

Talking points

- Do you have a church choir? If not, do you have a group of parishioners with sufficient interest to produce a choir?

- Is there someone who could help and direct them? Would there be cost implications?

- Can young people get to a choir practice, given the transport problems of a rural parish?

- Why not establish a drama group? Would the group perform in church? Could the drama group offer fund-raising occasions?

- Could drama be used as a vehicle for learning the stories of the bible, especially for young people?

- Could a drama group encourage young people to spend more leisure time in the parish?

29 Raising the profile

Press relations officer for parish

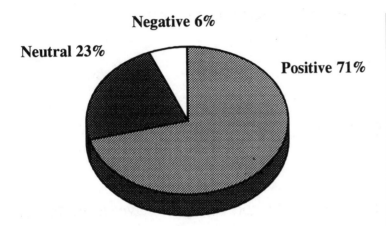

Negative 6%

Neutral 23%

Positive 71%

Positive 71%	
Church attendance	
Sometimes	65%
Weekly	74%
Age	
Under 50	74%
50-64	78%
65 and over	63%
Sex	
Male	73%
Female	70%

Be on the parish council

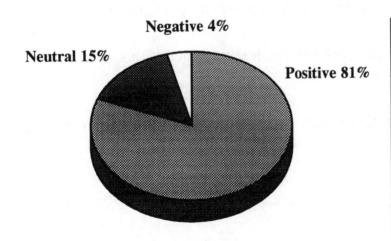

Negative 4%

Neutral 15%

Positive 81%

Positive 81%	
Church attendance	
Sometimes	76%
Weekly	84%
Age	
Under 50	82%
50-64	85%
65 and over	77%
Sex	
Male	82%
Female	81%

Listening to the statistics

- Over two thirds (71%) of rural churchgoers are positive about a lay person being press relations officer for the parish, although almost a quarter are indifferent.

- Regular churchgoers are somewhat more positive than occasional churchgoers about a lay person being press relations officer for the parish.

- Senior churchgoers are less convinced about a lay person being press relations officer for the parish than are younger churchgoers.

- Men and women hold similar attitudes to a lay person being press relations officer for the parish.

- Eight in ten rural churchgoers are supportive of a lay member being on the parish council.

- Regular churchgoers are somewhat more positive than occasional churchgoers about a lay member being on the parish council.

- All age groups are strongly supportive of a lay member being on the parish council.

- Men and women are equally positive about a lay member being on the parish council.

Reflection

There are many benefits in rural areas from church and local council working together. Each performs a service to the local people and they are more effective when not in opposition. What is more, the potential for regional aid and grants for building repairs are often best explored through local councillors.

Rural churches are often not skilled at gaining a good profile in the local press. Indeed, most ecclesiastical news that reaches the newspapers is bad news for the church. In the hands of the right lay people, much can be done to raise the media profile of the local church. Most churches have much to be proud of and do well to spread the good news as widely as possible.

'I see on page 12 that the Queen is visiting the town.'

Activity

Undertake a review of how the local press has reported your church in the recent past. Make a display of press cuttings in the church. Then list the other news which you would have liked to see in the local paper. Try writing some of this news in the style of the local paper.

Talking points

•   Are your Sunday church services, and other church events, advertised in the free press?

•   Would the church benefit from a more prominent profile in the local press?

•   Would more people come to church services if they knew more about their local church?

•   Would non-churchgoers feel better disposed towards the church if they heard more on local radio about what it stood for and why?

•   Can links between the church and community and parish councils be strengthened? How would both parties benefit?

•   Should parish/community council chairpersons be encouraged to hold inaugural services in church?

•   What are the pros and cons of the church being seen to be active in local politics?

30 Relating to the wider church

Official link with nearby parishes

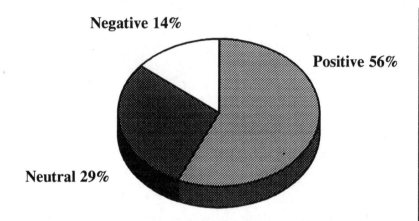

Negative 14%

Positive 56%

Neutral 29%

Positive 56%	
Church attendance	
Sometimes	48%
Weekly	61%
Age	
Under 50	59%
50-64	59%
65 and over	53%
Sex	
Male	58%
Female	56%

Represent parish on Synod

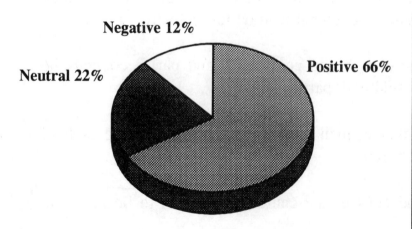

Negative 12%

Neutral 22%

Positive 66%

Positive 66%	
Church attendance	
Sometimes	50%
Weekly	74%
Age	
Under 50	60%
50-64	72%
65 and over	64%
Sex	
Male	70%
Female	63%

Listening to the statistics

- Many more churchgoers hold a positive view (56%) of lay people being the official link with nearby parishes than hold a negative view (14%).

- Regular churchgoers are more in favour than occasional churchgoers of lay people being the official link with nearby parishes.

- Those aged sixty-five and over are slightly less certain than younger churchgoers about lay people being the official link with nearby parishes.

- Men and women share a similar view on lay people being the official link with nearby parishes.

- Two thirds (66%) of rural church members are positive about lay people representing the parish on Synod.

- Regular churchgoers are much more enthusiastic than occasional churchgoers in their support for lay people representing the parish on Synod.

- The highest level of support for lay people representing the parish on Synod comes from those aged between fifty and sixty-four.

- Men are somewhat more supportive than women of lay people representing the parish on Synod.

Reflection

Although rural churches tend to be linked within multi-parish benefices, there is often still a need to build up closer cooperation between churches in the same benefice or deanery. Different parishes, even neighbouring parishes, may have different church traditions and their incumbents may have different views with regard to issues like the remarriage of divorced persons, the baptism of babies from non-churchgoing families, or the priesthood of women. Clearly, when official links ignore such sensitivities, difficulties could follow.

**'Psst...the Vicar says he's the new official link person
with the neighbouring parish—or, come to think of it, did he say 'missing
link?'**

Activity

Invite the parish representative to the deanery synod, the ruridecanal conference, or other inter-parish group to provide a display of the recent issues which have been discussed. How aware are most churchgoers of these issues?

Talking points

•   What would the official link person with a neighbouring parish actually do? With whom would they liaise in the neighbouring parish(es)?

•   What benefits might accrue from having a lay person act as official link with neighbouring parishes?

•   Do lay people who serve on the General Synod or the Governing Body represent themselves or the parish?

•   How are lay representatives on the General Synod or the Governing Body briefed before a meeting of Synod or Governing Body? How are they debriefed after a meeting?

Bibliography

Being Human, Being Church, Robert Warren, (1995) Marshall Pickering.

When I Needed a Neighbour – enabling pastoral care in the local church, Penny Nairne, (1998) Marshall Pickering.

Practising Community – the task of the local church, Robin Greenwood, (1996) SPCK.

Models of the Church, Avery Dulles, (1983) Dublin, Gill and Macmillan.

Total Ministry, Stewart Zabriskie, (1995) Alban Institute.

The Empowering Church, David Foy Crabtree, (1992) Alban Institute.

Power to the Powerless – theology brought to life, Laurie Green, (1987) Marshall Pickering.

Let's Do Theology, Laurie Green, (1990) Mowbray.

The Monday Connection, William E Diehl, (1991) Harper Collins.

Called To New Life – the world of lay discipleship, GS Misc 546, National Society.

The Servant Church – organising rural community care, Elfrida Savigear, (1995) ACORA.

Rural Praise – a parish workbook for worship in the country church, Francis and Martineau, (1996) Gracewing.

Ministry and Priesthood, A Redfern, (1999) London, Darton, Longman and Todd.

God's Here and Now - social contexts of the ministry and people of God, P Richter, (1999) London, Darton, Longman and Todd.

Living Theology, M West, G Noble and A Todd, (1999) London, Darton, Longman and Todd.

Appendix

The questionnaire which gathered the data used in this book is on the following two pages.

PART ONE What is your attitude toward lay people (other than Readers) with appropriate training and accreditation (where appropriate) carrying out the following functions? Please assess each issue by drawing a circle around one number between 1 and 5.

1 means very negative   3 means neutral   5 means very positive

Administer rotas	1 2 3 4 5	Visit elderly in residential homes	1 2 3 4 5
Church primary school governor	1 2 3 4 5	Funeral of church person	1 2 3 4 5
Take communion to the sick	1 2 3 4 5	Official link with nearby parishes	1 2 3 4 5
Read lessons at evensong	1 2 3 4 5	Visit the sick at home	1 2 3 4 5
Chair church council meeting	1 2 3 4 5	Run a mid-week children's club	1 2 3 4 5
Give out notices	1 2 3 4 5	Prepare those to be married	1 2 3 4 5
Contact newcomers in parish	1 2 3 4 5	Preach at the communion service	1 2 3 4 5
Arrange the flowers in church	1 2 3 4 5	Funeral of non-church person	1 2 3 4 5
Preach at matins or evensong	1 2 3 4 5	Baptise infants	1 2 3 4 5
Teach in Sunday school	1 2 3 4 5	Lock and unlock the church	1 2 3 4 5
Lead prayers at communion	1 2 3 4 5	Represent parish on Synod	1 2 3 4 5
Keep the parish records	1 2 3 4 5	Press relations officer for parish	1 2 3 4 5
Preach at a major festival	1 2 3 4 5	Minute church council meetings	1 2 3 4 5
Lead youth work	1 2 3 4 5	Record church covenants	1 2 3 4 5
Visit members of congregation	1 2 3 4 5	Organise church social program	1 2 3 4 5
Arrange special worship occasion	1 2 3 4 5	Be on the parish council	1 2 3 4 5
Pray for people in the parish	1 2 3 4 5	Organise care scheme in village	1 2 3 4 5
Visit bereaved before the funeral	1 2 3 4 5	Duplicate the church magazine	1 2 3 4 5
Oversee church security	1 2 3 4 5	Make bread for holy communion	1 2 3 4 5
Prepare adults for confirmation	1 2 3 4 5	Take care of church embroidery	1 2 3 4 5
Chair church school governors	1 2 3 4 5	Sing in the church choir	1 2 3 4 5
Choose hymns/songs for worship	1 2 3 4 5	Wind the church clock	1 2 3 4 5
Administer chalice at communion	1 2 3 4 5	Perform in church drama group	1 2 3 4 5
Read the Gospel at communion	1 2 3 4 5	Clean the communion vessels	1 2 3 4 5
Teach about baptism	1 2 3 4 5	Launder the church linen	1 2 3 4 5
Preside at the eucharist	1 2 3 4 5	Ring the church bells	1 2 3 4 5
Announce hymns	1 2 3 4 5	Organise lunch club for elderly	1 2 3 4 5
Clean the church	1 2 3 4 5	Serve coffee after the service	1 2 3 4 5
Edit the parish magazine	1 2 3 4 5	Play organ or other instruments	1 2 3 4 5
Hold confidential conversation	1 2 3 4 5	Welcome visitors and tourists	1 2 3 4 5
Visit bereaved after the funeral	1 2 3 4 5	Clean the choir surplices	1 2 3 4 5
Give address at family service	1 2 3 4 5	Organise concerts	1 2 3 4 5
Conduct the service at evensong	1 2 3 4 5	Distribute the magazine	1 2 3 4 5
Church visitor to primary school	1 2 3 4 5	Organise fundraising	1 2 3 4 5
Cut the churchyard grass	1 2 3 4 5	Prepare children for confirmation	1 2 3 4 5
Visit parishioners in hospital	1 2 3 4 5	County primary school governor	1 2 3 4 5
Lead a house discussion group	1 2 3 4 5	Administer bread at communion	1 2 3 4 5
Lead intercessions at communion	1 2 3 4 5	County primary school assembly	1 2 3 4 5
Church primary school assembly	1 2 3 4 5		

Age group

Under 20	1	
20 - 34	2	
35 - 49	3	
50 - 64	4	
65 and over	5	

Sex

Male	1	
Female	2	

Denomination

None	1	
Church of England	2	
Roman Catholic	3	
Free Church	4	
Other (specify)	5	

Church attendance

weekly	4	
at least monthly	3	
sometimes	2	
never	1	

Where you normally worship

village	4	
market town	3	
urban	2	
suburban	1	

Personal prayer

daily	4	
at least weekly	3	
Sometimes	2	
Never	1	

Please answer the following questions by putting a circle around the **'YES'** or the **'NO'**. Do not think too long about the exact meaning of the questions.

Does your mood often go up and down?	YES NO
Are you a talkative person?	YES NO
Would being in debt worry you?	YES NO
Are you rather lively?	YES NO
Were you ever greedy by helping yourself to more than your share of anything?	YES NO
Would you take drugs which may have strange or dangerous effects?	YES NO
Have you ever blamed someone for doing something you knew was really your fault?	YES NO
Do you prefer to go your own way rather than act by the rules?	YES NO
Do you often feel 'fed-up'?	YES NO
Have you ever taken anything (even a pin or button) that belonged to someone else?	YES NO
Would you call yourself a nervous person?	YES NO
Do you think marriage is old-fashioned and should be done away with?	YES NO
Can you easily get some life into a rather dull party?	YES NO
Are you a worrier?	YES NO
Do you tend to keep in the background on social occasions?	YES NO
Does it worry you if you know there are mistakes in your work?	YES NO
Have you ever cheated at a game?	YES NO
Do you suffer from 'nerves'?	YES NO
Have you ever taken advantage of someone?	YES NO
Are you mostly quiet when you are with other people?	YES NO
Do you often feel lonely?	YES NO
Is it better to follow society's rules than go your own way?	YES NO
Do other people think of you as being very lively?	YES NO
Do you always practise what you preach?	YES NO